Signature Collection

Maxine Spyres Hixon

Signature Collection

Maxine Spyres Hixon

Published by:
Brentwood Christian Press
P. O. Box 4773
Columbus, Georgia 31914-4773
(800) 334-8861
www.brentwoodbooks.com

Poetry Collections by Maxine:

Sand and Pearls
Voice of the Heart
Poetic Potpourri
Mither
Rhymes of the Time (children's book – a collaborative work with her daughters)
Hidden Treasure I
Hidden Treasure 11
Hidden Treasure 111
Wealth of Wisdom

One of Maxine's favorite Bible scripture verses:

Deuteronomy 31:6

*"Be strong and of a good courage,
fear not, nor be afraid of them:
For the Lord thy God, he it is that doth go with thee;
he will not fail thee, nor forsake thee."*

Table of Contents

SALVATION

COMFORT, HOPE and INSPIRATION

DOCTRINAL and DIDACTIC

SEASONAL and OCCASIONAL

NATURE

POETIC FORMS

THOUGHT-PROVOKING

POLITICAL

NOSTALGIA and ROMANCE
(Cinquains & Triolets)

HOME and FAMILY

ECLECTIC

In Loving Memory

Foreword

It's so easy for us to write and sing our Mother's praises! She was such a God-fearing soul with a tender, compassionate heart, spun of pure gold. Besides being the best Mother in the world to which we can affirm, Dad attested to her being the best helpmeet and wife in their sixty-one year marriage. We think Proverbs, chapter 31, fitly describes her.

She not only possessed a keen intelligence, she also possessed wisdom from God to go with it, and shared that wisdom with all the people who were fortunate enough to cross her path. Dad always preached that wisdom (a gift from God) meant using the knowledge gained for the benefit of yourself and others. Mother did just that. She shares with you in this volume of poetry, her *"Signature Collection,"* the wisdom she gained through her years of serving the Lord, and a lifetime of being about her Master's business. So it is a real privilege to be in her company as you read to uncover the great spiritual truths within the following pages.

Maxine had a deep love for lost souls, for she understood the great value of a soul, and she knew each soul is precious in God's eyes, bespoken by Calvary's love.

Maxine's tombstone is inscribed "Victory in Jesus" which was one of her favorite songs, also. She knew our earthly pilgrimage was one in which we are just "passing through," and that her treasures were laid up in Heaven in that land "beyond the blue."

She is numbered with the Saints of old, for she truly lived a life dedicated to the Lord's service and left behind an exemplary personal testimony. When she stands in her lot at the end of time, we know she will be among the greatest to have

13

ever lived. We know, for a truth, she has had great influence over her children's lives, and if one star shines brightest under God's great firmament, it will be Mother's, for she turned many to God's saving grace, to truth and to righteousness.

Selfless love, an undaunted formidable spirit, an unwavering faith in her Lord, and a courageous heart bespeak her. One of her favorite scriptures was, "Be of good courage, and the Lord will strengthen your heart."

And so we present this priceless writing by our Mother who left this great legacy behind for everyone. It can be said with a certainty, she was "ever true to God." These words need to be inscribed for posterity, for Maxine set her affections on things above, and hence when she went to be with Jesus on December 2, 2006, she changed her place of abode, but not her company. The best thing that could ever be said to each of her children, was "Mother's been praying for you," for her prayers had power with God, and reached to the Throne of God's love, mercy and grace.

No one has been left behind to take up Mother's mantle of blessing like Elijah and Elisha in days of old, as the Bible records. She is the only one. After her lifetime, the mold has been broken. But, we can honestly say writing about her has been one of the easiest things we've ever done, for our hearts just overflow with her praises. May you, too, be blessed by her life, is our prayer.

We know what Mother would say, "If only one soul was saved by her life's example, telling souls how to be saved, it would be worth a lifetime and all of her writing endeavors." For all the angels of Heaven will rejoice over that lost soul that was found.

No one can ever fill her shoes, but they can follow in her footsteps, which will lead to the Savior, the Lord Jesus Christ, and Heaven's bright eternal home.

It wouldn't be a fair assessment of Mother's individuality, without telling of how she lived an abundant life – the kind the Lord tells us He came to give. Maxine enjoyed the works of her hands, as did Solomon, of the Bible. This ability to enjoy life, affected all who knew her, and "her sense of having fun" became contagious. This keen insight into humanity, helps to make even heavy burdens light. She always sang while working in the kitchen – cooking up something absolutely delicious for her family. This is a memory we have that is absolutely priceless.

Blessed were the lives of those who knew her, and may you, too, receive a blessing for having met her through her poetry. Her poetry was "destined" to be shared.

You will find at the close of this collection, a poem each that we her daughters have written for Mother. We hope you enjoy them.

So until we all meet in Heaven's fair day,

Maxine's two daughters,

Tena M. Hixon and Pamela Hixon Rhea

Biography

Maxine Spyres was born on January 29, 1926 in Adair County, Stilwell, Oklahoma.

She was valedictorian of her eighth grade class, and finished high school a year early. She married Carl W. Hixon on October 6, 1945 in Selma, California. They have four children: Tena, Pamela, Ronald, and Rodney.

Maxine attended the Northeastern State Teacher's College in Tahlequah, Oklahoma. She taught school during World War II in a one-room schoolhouse – children of all ages.

Maxine's collection of inspirational poetry published in recent years are *Sand and Pearls, Voice of the Heart, Mither,* (a collection of one hundred twenty-two poems, written in its entirety after Maxine suffered a left-side paralysis stroke,) *Poetic Potpourri, Hidden Treasure (Volumes 1 and 11, & 111,) Wealth of Wisdom* and this, her *Signature Collection.* In 1995, Maxine collaborated with her two daughters, to write a children's book, *Rhymes of the Times* published in 2015, which she illustrated.

Maxine's poems have been published in her hometown *Log Cabin Democrat* for over thirty-eight years. Many of her poems have won prizes in poetry contests, been published in anthologies, and are on the Internet.

Maxine and her family made their home in Conway, Arkansas, for over thirty-eight years, where her two daughters continue to reside.

This volume, *Signature Collection,* completes 8 volumes of religious poetry, not including the children's rhyme book, and the book, *Mither,* written after having a stroke. Maxine passed from this life on, December 2, 2006, exactly seven months and seven days after suffering her massive stroke. Her daughters have published her works posthumously.

Her works will continue live on in the hearts and minds of her many readers, whose lives will be made richer for the reading.

Salvation

Being Thankful

Salvation is a gift to all who accept Christ as
    Saviour.
Through repentance and faith, a person is
    saved –;
Knowing Christ as Saviour is the way to
    God's favor …
When Jesus was crucified … Salvation's price
    was paid.

Though Salvation is a gift offered to
    all …
One must accept Christ … that's where security
    for eternity doth lie –;
A sacrifice for sin was needed
    after man's fall;
In the Garden of Eden, Adam and Eve
    disobeyed God … having to die.

Just as one can reject Christ … refusing
    Salvation –;
So can we, after Salvation … not rightly evaluate
    God's blessings … and continually mope.
If headlong our own way … and God's admonition
    we shun …;
Nor acknowledge the many blessings … for thankfulness
    there's no hope.

Do we accept God's great Salvation as a
    gift ...
Then refuse to take note of a multitude
    of blessings He gives –;
Hanging on ... refusing to allow Him life's burdens
    to lift;
And ignoring all good things God provides ...
    as one lives.

Every good and perfect gift is from ...
    above;
Many times taking for granted God's
    blessings, yet thinking so thoughtlessly overlooked ...
His blessings are sent – not because
    we're worthy – but, because of love.
Only through Christ can we belong to God ... one belonging
    to Him, He has never forsaken.

God's Plan

For God so loved all of us ... the whole
    world ...;

He gave His Son, Jesus, to be crucified on
    Calvary for our sin –;

When Adam and Eve transgressed in the garden
    of Eden ... the world into sin was hurled.

Jesus wouldn't have needed to come and die to
    save our soul ... if another way there'd been.

An all-knowing, all-powerful God in His great
    wisdom ... does nothing in vain ...;

It's sinful man and his vanity who is determined
    to make ... his own plan –;

When man makes his own plan for Salvation ...
    God's plan he disdains;

Since God has no beginning or end ... it's a shame
    that sinful ... weak, finite, dispensable man,
      seeks – in salvation to give God a hand.

Happiness or Joy

Everyone likes to be happy – no one likes to
    be sad ...
Happiness doesn't depend upon outward circumstances
    sent –;
Money is the factor some gauge happiness
    by ... a longing to be had –;
They're so busy ... planning how to gain something
    more – will never relent.

Joy comes from deep within, the spirit – the very
    heart of man ...
It never ... leaves the heart – it's forever
    there to stay –;
Circumstances make no difference – joy
    from the heart is constant – material things have
    no hand –;
Accepting Christ as Saviour ... will make
    for a joyous day.

Because of Love

God so loved the world ... He gave His
  Only begotten Son ...
Christ so loved the Father ... He willingly
  became the sacrificial one.
Such love ... unsought and unmerited, by
  the human race;
We love Him because He first loved
  us ... Oh, His matchless wondrous grace.

What a terrible thought that we should trample
  underfoot the love of God –;
Man's determined to have his own way ... when
  only made from the dust ... akin to the sod.
So dependent are we ... for our sustenance, even the
  air we breathe ...
Yet, if things don't go to plan, we childishly
  pout and are peeved.

Patient is our Lord ... with His erring
  child.
Yet, to be pleasing to Him, we must
  become as a child ...
If you would please God, have faith, ... for without it,
  it's impossible to do.
Repentance and faith ... the way ... necessary –
  the two.

God's love encompasses ... His whole
    creation ...
From none does He withhold His love –
    mattering not, whether a high or lowly station.
God reacts to man as man reacts to God;
Drawing closer to Him ... man feels less,
    the "chastening rod."

So Busy

Are we so obsessed with failings of others ...
We fail to recognize – failings of our
    own –;
Becoming so critical – looking past ourselves
    to another ...
When criticism – should stay closer
    to home.

Self-improvement can never be ...
    with your obsession to improve on me –;
Turn it around ... the same proves
    true, my first priority isn't to improve on you.
If I've only uppermost in mind – your improvement –
    a mistake to see ...
Improvement to truly come about –
    you work on you – I work on me –let's do!

True change can only come ... through
    Christ ...
When heart is changed – made new
    in Salvation –;
Accepting God's gift ... His Son – without
    price ...
Yet, free to all – who will in faith partake –
    not mine, but Thy will be done.

Good-bye To Self

It's appointed unto man once to die
And after this the judgment …
At that time, earthly life will have passed on by
Your Spirit either to Heaven went or to Hell your Spirit
sent.

Either way, it's good-bye to self as you know it.
The body returns to the dust in time.
We were put on earth to worship God, but
man forgets,
And walks with the devil in perfect rhyme.

In time, we'll say good-bye to this earthly life.
What have you if you gain the whole world,
but lose your own soul?
If you think this life is nothing but strife …
Hell's a fire burning with torment forever
in God's word we're told.

God sent His Son to die … for our "escape."
He took our place on Calvary's rugged Cross
He died for us while his tormentors gaped.
In Salvation, Christ's blood removed sin's dross.

Salvation is by grace … through faith in Christ.
It doesn't come through works man has done.
Christ came to save … He is the only One
One must accept the Saviour … God's own Son.

Faith Instead of "Why"

Man is of few days and full of trouble the Bible states …
Yet, with heartache and a sigh asking, "Why" when it's
  nigh.
It rains on the just and unjust as for the showers we await;
God in His power and wisdom rules from His throne on
  high.

As Christ was crucified upon the cross …
He said "My God, my God, why hast thou forsaken me,"
As He suffered such pain for our sin and dross;
God didn't answer Jesus' cry of "why" … knowing He
  heard, one can't deny.

But, when Christ died fulfilling His appointed mission,
Rocks rent, an earthquake, darkness covered the earth, the
  sun refused to shine.
God is sovereign … doesn't have to account for "why" to
  any decision;
Faith is trust and belief in God … no answer when asked,
  "why" you find.

What Is It Then?

Down through time, God's men have preached …
The ones God called … the lost to reach –;
Since Christ organized His Church on the shores of Galilee;
There's been faithful followers, preaching to help set souls
    free.

Preaching God's Word, telling of His saving grace …
Of how Jesus was sent to die for the human race –;
How He died on Calvary's rugged cross;
Saving all who would believe in Him… overcoming sin's
    dross.

The Apostle Paul made tents, and yet … preached …
Down through the ages others have worked, to be able to
    preach and teach;
The gifts and callings of God are without repentance –;
After a hard day's work … on God's Word they took their
    stance.

Now, in time as we know it … this "modern time" …
It seems many choose to listen to stories or rhymes;
God's promise is, the Holy Spirit will accompany His Word;
To the convicting of those who hear … or have heard.

What is it then … when multitudes come forward …
When scant, if any scripture is used to MAR their MODERN
    (gospel?);
To be saved one must believe what Jesus taught while here on
    earth;
By grace through faith in Him is Salvation or the New
    Birth.

As the tree falleth … so shall it lie …;
We are, as we are, when to earth we've said "goodbye";
Today is the day of Salvation … now is the accepted time–;
Though God is long-suffering, His love … with judgment
    is combined.

Salvation is by repentance and faith in Christ …;
When Christ died, He paid Salvation's price –;
People who wait for a, "great gathering" their faith to state;
Much publicity at any rate … but, after death … too late
    the state of
                    The
                        Soul
                            To
                                Debate!!!

31

Dear Jesus
(A Prayer for children and everyone)

Dear Jesus,

You were a dear little lamb,
You died on the cross for all the lost,
Please forgive me – help me to live
So I can go to Heaven to live with
You when I die.

To a little lamb was Jesus likened.
His spirit was – meek as a lamb
He died for all – on Calvary's cross
To remove from hearts all sin's dross.
We must accept the sacrifice given,
If we would go to live with Him in Heaven.

A lamb is so lovable,
It is such an innocent little thing.
Helpless to do for itself at all
Quietly gamboling on the hills to fall.
Needs much care and looking after
The Shepherd faithful – saving from hell's hereafter.

Comfort, Hope and Joy

The Only Hope

It was recently said ... we read – concerning the
    meaning of hope ... "new hope" –;
Nothing is new – though experienced by many
    or few ... of the, " hope" in Christ ...
Repentance is a must – in God's sight to be
    just – and Christ as Saviour you need trust;
It's all of faith ... not by works of righteousness –
    the, "only hope" God's plan – yet, many resist!

To each person of the sod – just trusting Christ
    through the plan of God – it is only, "new" ...
Man has placed his hope in God's plan ... shortly
    after the creation of man ... continues to stand;
Adam and Eve were the first – after their transgression
    in the Garden of Eden ... and numbers grew –;
Christ for the Salvation of the soul of man –
    from the "Covenant Halls" of eternity – God's plan.

Hope is the promise for the future – trust does nurture
    with faith enabling to speak boldly;
Hope not being left to the ... vain ability
    (disability) or devise of man ...
To have hope in this life only –we're of all
    men most miserable – said the Apostle Paul, of old;
There's an, "All-Seeing Eye" – nothing does
    escape ... of what transpires through ALL the land.

Light

Early morning and noonday sun ...
How strong and glorious in its ascension;
With no voice ... shining on all ... yet, for none;
Mindlessly keeping the decreed course to run.

In creation, God said, " Let there be light";
The sun to rule by day ...
The moon and stars to rule by night;
Shining only by God's force from on high.

Earthly life impossible without God's gift of light;
The sun's attributes everywhere are sung ...
Giving light and warmth before the night;
God in His infinite wisdom and love placed the sun.

The sun – no strength its own ... without reason or sense;
Unwavering ... without decision on its certain path ...
On a course of God's benevolence –
Our great God has divested ... all that it hath.

Though weak, man has voice unlike the powerful sun;
God gave man power to choose ... changing his course ...
He chooses his own path as life's race he runs.
Christ is the Light of the world ... Salvation's source.

God sent Jesus, the Light of the world ...
To die at Calvary ... for man's sin.
When Adam and Eve transgressed, the world into sin was
    hurled.
The light ... God's word tells of Christ, the Heavenly Light ...
    came to save the souls of men.

Above the Gloom and Fray

A dark, cloudy, rainy day sets one to thinking in dismal
　　gloom …;
Thinking not of now … reaching in time, that's to be
　　soon, when spirit will rise, visualizing flowers in bloom.
It takes the rain … as well the sun, for beauty not
　　surpassed by painter one.
Each day thirsty soil embraces rain and sun, while
　　beauty lies hidden, in time nature's beauty is sung.
A dejected sprit can cause gloom … to a life as well
　　as a frayed heart;
Aside from troubles, which come to all … much to visualize
　　for the future … but, prayer is where to start.

God has so blessed, giving us a beautiful place from
　　birth to live and dwell on earth;
Loved ones and friends to fill our homes and lives
　　with happiness and mirth.
Our passage from this life to Heaven, Christ on Calvary
　　has already bought …
If we will only accept Him as our own Saviour … as in the
　　Bible we're so plainly taught –
We can live with Him in Heaven where dwells no gloom …
　　beauty is forever bright.
No gloom to mar … all joy, peace and light … no need for
　　the sun, for God's Son is Heaven's Light.

Why Worry?

Why should man worry about what is God's business ...;
When we fail in that ... our own –;
We worry and fret while blessings we miss ... yet, still resist
To obey and follow our Lord ... while evil is condoned.

God spoke the universe into existence ...;
Finished His creation according to His own plan;
Finite, sinful man, in obeying God ... has always given
    resistance.
First, Adam and Eve, in the Garden of Eden, then sin covered
    the land.

Why do we not rest secure in God's care and wisdom ...
When not one sparrow falls without His knowing –;
For He is omnipresent, omnipotent, omniscient.;
Yet, man away from God ... seems always to be going.

God placed the planets ... millions of stars in the sky are sown;
Not only did He place them there, but, knows them all by name ...
Since even the stars to Him are known, all evil comes before
    His Throne.
God's power in Heaven ... and on earth, the same.

God has no starting place … no beginning or end …;
He gave Christ, His Son, the Sacrificial Lamb – the Great I Am.
God, from eternity (like a circle) to eternity … has no end.
He holds the key to Hell … where lost souls are damned.

God's plan is through Christ … for many to escape Hell …;
By accepting Him as Saviour … Heaven is gained –;
A place prepared by Christ where all the redeemed will dwell.
Man makes his choice, God giving him voice – life isn't a game.

Without Doubt

After your pray and do all the things – God
   would have you do …
You must wait while God works things out –
   on the other side…
The Bible tells us to – wait upon the
   Lord – to wait … is hard for me and you.
He is the One in charge – we must in faith –
   pray His Will be done – then by it abide.

Wait on the Lord – as He in His perfection –
   works things out …
We're not to be overanxious – but, trust –
   we're in His Hands –;
It is He who allows things to be … but,
   when He is ready, a halt He'll call about.
Evil can only have its effect – within the
   realm – as God allows with man.

God is all-powerful – we have access to
   Him – through Christ in prayer –.
We're in comparison … as only an ant –
   so small – easily overlooked, by all.
God gives strength to face the devil and
   every problem – when with faith we do and dare.
Yet, God always hears us when with broken
   hearts on Him we call.

Burdens are too heavy for one so weak …
   when burdened down with care;
But, we have a Heavenly Father and Christ,
   our Saviour, to carry us safely through –;
With help from above… we're in His care –
   He'll never allow us more than we can bear.
Other of God's people offering their help because
 of love – your courage will renew.

Feeling Bad!

Feeling bad … everything seems so
    slow –
You just can't speed things up, wanting
    to, even though.
All things seem – such a –
    chore –.
Things enjoyed doing – always –
    before.
Just need patience – everything's such
    a bore.
Praying is the best thing for all this I
    know;
To lift you out of the rut in the –
    road.
Discouragement comes when you open the
    door.
So never give way – keep pity at –
    bay.
Not saying you don't feel bad –
    today;
With God's help, we don't have to stay
    that way.
When you feel you're slipping –
    apart;
Kneeling somewhere is the best place to
    start.

Though to pray, the position's not the
   necessary part;
It's us relating to God what's in our –
   heart.
Life can be good, even when things look
   dark.
Feeling bad? Keep looking up, faith the
   doldrums disrupt.
Soon, with God's thoughts "from His Book"
   … things will be looking up.

Lack of Trust

There are many people who are so adverse;
Everything they're told, they must do differently;
They'll tell you they know best about everything;
It matters not how far from right ... though they see!

They fail to show real interest in anything!
Seeing no possibilities, in whatever's done;
Continue to let opportunities pass by ...
Procrastinating, aiming, only at life's fun.

Never had anything and seemingly never will!
For want of responsibility and frivolous things;
Necessities expected from someone else!
They lack faith and ambition which trust will bring.

It is said, "the Lord helps those, who help themselves".
The Lord does say, "If you don't work, you don't eat!"
And, "Without faith, it's impossible to please God."
Christ as your Saviour, brings the devil's defeat.

God's promises to man are sure and steadfast;
He never leaves us once we belong to Him;
In disobedience, we may turn from what is right!
Without repentance, backsliding – with one's faith growing
   dim.

ALL ... who are the Lord's will receive chastisement;
For the Lord will chasten ALL those who are His;
Because of His great love, He brings us closer;
His chastisement means love, that's the way it is!

It's so sad if you be without chastisement!
When one knows Christ as Saviour, he still will sin;
If there's no chastening, you're a bastard, not His;
No one's perfect, ALL do sin ... not IF, but, when!

There are many people who are so adverse;
Everything they're told, they must do differently;
They'll tell you they know best about everything;
Matters not, what the Bible says ... just won't see.

Belated Thank You

To see someone stand – for that which is
   right …
Encourages others to Christ, to prove faithful
   and true;
Not only does their testimony – make for
   endurance … but is, to hearts, a delight –;
Many times when right is presented bold …
   a multitude chooses right, to hold – evil to eschew.

Too seldom do we take time, to think … thanking
   God for those who from persecution – didn't shrink;
There are those living on earth today … who
   for right are willing to pay …
Many Christians of old – to the devil didn't sell
   their souls … with martyrdom on the brink –.
In Biblical days – the apostles of old – with
   allegiance to the Lord their goal – their faith did stay.

Such examples for us to read … many lives –
   we need to heed;
Increase our faith we need to pray … as Christ
   taught His disciples in Biblical days –;
Why should we who stand for right –
   believe always to have the easiest of plights? …
So let's thank God for those before – who
   against evil stood the more – letting God direct
    their ways.

If we let our minds – directed by
    God – dwell on examples in the past;
Our lives would be more fruitful –
    lived more abundantly – and peace indwell –;
Thanksgiving to God for all His blessings …
    Salvation through Christ – does eternally last …
When living for Christ … others can
    see – a life force other than ourselves …
        not an empty shell.

One Among Many

Isn't there enough hurt ... without you adding more?
Someone burdened down ... do you just ignore?
Are you so self-centered – and continue to think ...
You're the only one ... and with wisdom to the brink;
Others have troubles with heartache a plenty ...
Each person is only ONE ... a number in many.

Never refuse to help or speak words of comfort ...
Being careful of harshness ... not necessarily curt;
Try to help those who continue to struggle –;
Their life in disarray ... a terrible muddle ...;
Many a worse condition than you're in ... to be found;
Faith and trust in the Lord makes for heart and
     mind that's sound.

Misconception

Do you ever in haste … misjudge – interpret incorrectly,
    yet, hold a deep-seated grudge …
So determined to have things your way … no matter if
    justice is held at bay –,
When holding a grudge … one fails to be fair … acting
    the judge;
You reap what you sow … another day … high-handed
    unfairness, does never pay.

The devil … wherever he can … delights in turning any
    life upside-down;
With blinders, he covers the truth … being a master at
    confusion's game –;
Everywhere people do exist … the devil does persist and
    lurk around …;
His business is to destroy personal testimony and lives, being the
    author of sin … if doing his bidding we are to blame.

As a people, we are prone to sin … our failings are many,
    … each and everyone –;
We're prone to use a magnifying glass … when looking at
    the lives of others –;
But, never … until we turn the glass upon ourselves … is
    the job rightly done;
We're all subject to sin and failings … falling short of
    God's perfection – the same as our sisters and our brothers.

Is It Was Or Was It Ain't?

Did you ever do a certain thing
   not right;
That is false, for there's no ...
   feeling of guilt,
An extended relationship or
   fight ...
No matter the evidence that
   has built?

Is it true ... past or present, did
   or do;
If it's false .. "is it was," or "was it
   ain't? ..."
"Yes," "no," "maybe so," "certainly's ...
   not true;"
The verb's where the action is ...
   "is it 'tis."

The English language has lost
   all meaning
Analyzing ... scrutinizing ...
   each word ...
"Did, do, done, is, was, were, are"... meaning plain;
Hey, that's insane ... many leanings
   to a verb!

Life has many crooks and
    turns – ups, and downs;
The journey is filled with "in
    turns" and "out,"
Truth always finds the "light"
    for which its bound;
With answers made plain, there
    remains no doubt.

"Give me a break," not hard to
    understand,
For words do have meanings,
    by rote we get;
Even crossword puzzles, meanings
    demand!
With word's true meaning, the
    picture is set.

Have we had a revision of our
    language,
That we can't tell "did" or "do" …
    "is" or "ain't"'
Is there nothing definite by
    which to gauge?
'Tis God who brings all things
    to light, not fate!

It has been said, "The
    wheels of God's judgment,
grind slowly … but, they grind
    exceedingly fine."

Out For Self!

Causing contention by tale-bearing and being unfair ...;
Telling tales untrue ... yet, never to rue –;
Stirring up strife ... to many isn't rare ...
Those to be peacemakers ... scarce and few.

To turn the attention away from you ...;
For many deeds done ... not right –;
Bring up anything you can ... that'll do;
Yet, sooner than later, truth is brought to light.

The guilty always have to run for cover and hide ...;
No ways to cope ... with Christ as hope, no measuring up.
For truth and right ... a coward won't abide ...;
Blackened hearts sup from sin's overflowing cup.

Condemnation of self ... always far away ...;
Trying to harm others – who're safe, "in the eye of the storm";
While you, intending wounded hearts to suffer and pay –;
And your disregard of truth causes sorrow and much alarm.

The Lord will protect His own ... His way ...;
His power unleashed in all its strength the world yet to see;
Uplifted by His love ... those trampled down won't stay –;
In the depths of despair ... but, with wings of a dove, fly free.

If one professes salvation ... to be a child of God;
And wrong continues ... lifelong ...;
With never having felt God's chastening rod –;
A professor ... not a possessor – the Bible says ... a bastard,
    not a son ... if never corrected for doing wrong.

If Christ truly lives ... in a heart ...;
There's condemnation for sin and falling short –;
For God's Holy Spirit always does His convicting part;
Conscience can become seared ... that's to be feared –
    becoming the devil's cohort.

Some no condemnation for wrong ever feel ...;
Conscience void of offense – where sin remains dense;
Out just for self – to God in humility won't kneel –;
In the Judgment it'll be too late – hence no defense.

Friend or Enemy?

Ah, friend! Why hast thou to enemy turned?
Or was I deceived, to just now have learned:
'Tis best to know, without hypocrisy ...
Can there be a question, now it is discerned!

When ill health kept that faltering ego low;
Surrounded by those you considered foe,
Watching to criticize what would be next;
Needing support with noose tightening on neck.

What changed, "friend" with success on ladder reached?
Ethics proclaimed for years, obviously breached!
That which was condemned in others before ...
Is now in the spotlight ... cannot ignore.

Sometimes, "the success' ladder" rises too high;
Truth left somewhere near the bottom or nigh;
The higher one climbs, the harder the fall,
Arrogance and pride ... ends in bitter gall.

Friends are more than, "rungs" to be stepped upon;
Lest when you come down, the "rungs" will be gone:
Headlong, many have fallen from their, "perch"!
Not seeing the "friends" ... though brazenly search.

"He who has friends must show himself friendly;"
This is so true ... for the Bible does teach:
"Friend," is someone on whom you can depend;
Even to "your" work, their back they do bend.

Promises made to get the advantage ...
Until one's goals are reached – friendship, the bridge:
When crossed to success' side, no more need;
So-called "friend" turns to enemy with speed.

So soon forgotten ... help that's gone before!
When goal seems reached ... presuming a touchdown
    score;
Penalties come when "game" isn't played right ...
Nothing hid from the "All-Seeing-Eye's" sight!

Ah, Friend! Why hast thou to enemy turned?
Or was I deceived, to just now have learned:
'Tis best to know, without hypocrisy ...
Can there be a question, now it is discerned!

Time Doesn't Change Everything

If what you do and what you say –;
Are as far apart as night and day ...
When we say ... what we'll do-;
To do what we say ... not something in lieu;
Not just talking with enthusiasm ...
But, to accomplish what's talked one should pursue;
Everyone ... not just a minority of a few ...
Detest a prevaricator with commitments he eschews.

"A man is as good as his word" ...
In olden times was as prevalent statement heard;
The, "axiom" which so many hearts stirred,
Was a cloak for many ... being staunchly gird –.
Values remain the same ... whatever the age;
They never take wing and fly as the bird ...
Long ago, a man was only as good as his word;
Thinking to change what's proved true through the annals
    of time, would be absurd !

Steady On

When troubles o'erwhelm you ... pressing you
   down ...
God's the only help for man ... still on His
   throne ... as before troubles began ...;
Faith causes one to trust in God ... no matter
   what surrounds;
With the eye of faith ... seeing what is not –
   while God's all-seeing-eye sees across the land.

When dark clouds and dense fog swirl, whirl ...
   mightily ... pulling down ...
Faith looks upward and seeth ... the beautiful
   Heavenly Home – bequest;
Sure footing on solid ground – never looking down,
   trusting God ... though to earth we're bound –;
Always soaring ... rising above adverse circumstances ...
   that's faith's bequest.

So many things in this life ... cause heartache ...
   sickness, disappointment and strife;
Enduring faith ... makes life's pathway show bright...
   shining forth with Heavenly light –;
It matters not ... we may forget the reason ... not even
   remember life or the season ...
The maniac of the Gadarenes – worshipped Jesus ...
   his healing – delivered from sin's mental dark
     night.

Sands of Time

The sands of time slowly trickle through –
   experiences – the hourglass of life …
Our time on earth is meted out by a loving
   God of power.
He watches each and everyone each minute,
   every hour.
His love for the world … caused Him to
   send His only begotten Son.

Christ came to die on Calvary to give His
   life for you and me.
Many through the sands of time – have taken
   advantage of the magnificent gift proffered.
If you desire a home in Heaven – you must
   accept the salvation, through Christ that's offered.
Refusing to choose Christ – your choice is made –
   the lake of fire – Christ the only way to be free!

The sands in the hour glass of time … swiftly
   trickle away …
A decision must be made concerning eternity –
   while the sands of life are running still …
After life has left the body … the spirit is
   either in Heaven or hell.
The grave only receives the body … while the
   spirit is held at bay …

The only way to make up for time wasted while
     here on earth we stay ...
Is to work – as the Bible tells us – to redeem the
     time – for evil are the days.
We are to serve the Lord ... to Him our lives
     and talents fully yield;
Trusting a loving – all-knowing Saviour,
     and with repentant hearts to pray.

Friend or Foe

Who's your friend ... do you know who
　　your enemy is?
Much of the time ... things are so different
　　than what they seem –;
Those who may pose as trusted
　　allies ...
In spite of all the superfluous evidence
　　showing otherwise ...

Do you know who the enemy is ...?
　　may be a wolf in sheep's clothing –
It isn't always the one who is outspoken
　　or meets you head-on –;
The hidden foe is more dangerous
　　and loathing ...
Be watchful – the devil has many tricks
　　he sets forth – promotes and loans!

The Life You Choose

Make the best of each day God gives;
You can't run away from life.
Death ... removes from all the lives;
Dividing ... more than the sharpest knife.

Unless you stop living ...
You're responsible for so much;
To God and others ... of our best giving;
A standard bearer ... for right is such.

Seeing beauty in that which surrounds;
Nothing for granted ever taken ...;
Manifold blessings are evidence that God's mercy abounds;
God's long-suffering ... should never be for indifference
    mistaken.

He takes note of every sparrow falling;
Nothing done escapes His view –;
Always ready when He hears us calling;
Trouble to His children is nothing new.

God's plan for man ... in the Bible unfolds ...;
Not traveling to "Baghdad"* ... blinded, nothing foretold –
Life is an adventure to the meek – faith making bold;
Coming to the Throne of God for His Arms to enfold.

Each pays the price for disobedience ... actions which the
    devil does assist.
Christ came that we might have a more abundant life –;
Accept Him as Saviour; God's gift no longer resist;
Death continues to march ... ears hearing strains of the fife.

* Baghdad: There was a story about a man from Baghdad, who had an encounter with death
at the marketplace, with death beckoning to him. He was scared and ran away, got on his
horse and rode to Samaria. Death explained how he was just as shocked to see the man in
Baghdad, for he had an appointment that night with him in "Samaria."

What Might Have Been

Reminiscing as to what has gone before ... can take
   up all our time ...;
While what's going passed us now ... is where
   our life begins –;
The future is never here ... the present swiftly
   passes, we find – ever to view ... must look behind;
Wasted time in looking back – unless to learn where
   we lack – life continues to spin ... years descend.

When you are prone to think "what might have been" –
   it's ... always for the better ...;
Look around you taking note ... many there are in
   a much worse, "boat" –;
God gave His only begotten Son on the cross that
   we might have salvation free ... no debtor be;
Christ came that we might have life and have it
   more abundantly – to Him our life we need devote.

Count your daily blessings ... as time goes by –
   catch it while you can ...;
Make the most of each day we live ... enjoy
   God's blessings ... only His to lend;
Soon the time that's present now will be in the
   past ... to only scan;
Forever, in neglecting what time is "now" we
   continue to live, "what might have been."

Haunting Memories

Memories may haunt you …
As you take a trip down Memory Lane,
If you had done this, instead of that;
Your memories wouldn't be the same!
So … the memories you have …;
…Are yours for keeps …!
What you put into memory's cache;
Is all you'll ever reap …!

Being careful as you gather –,
And fill your cache with song;
Then as you go down Memory Lane,
You can sing – happily along.
No dark shadows to haunt you;
While the sun shines on the lane;
And you've lined the walk with flowers,
Their fragrance – never the same!

Then, anytime you choose, my dear;
Just start strolling down the lane.
All the good memories put away;
Will on their own, go drifting about.
So make sure you fill … full …
The reservoir as best you can!
When memories are all that's left;
There'll be none to ban – no running out!

Happiness

Thinking back ... knowing now ... there was
    extreme happiness;
But, at the time – not realizing this, until
    everything changed.
Then to reminisce – on what was back then,
    hard to resist.
Not knowing, how circumstances will be ...
    rearranged;
Bringing, perhaps, heartache and sorrow –
    causing the eye to mist;
Cast to the depths of despair ... heartbroken ...
    mind deranged.

Until such unhappiness is experienced – one
    can't guess;
How happy you were before ... with life at
    its best.
Now having something by which to ...
    compare;
Knowing such weight of burdens – descending
    on shoulders to rest.
Doubtful things will ever be the same – happiness –,
    did exist back there.
Realizing this – after seeing more of life, with so
    many heartaches and tests.

Now, looking back as through life ... we
   pass;
As maturing and learning each day ... as we
   travel along;
Understanding better the need to enjoy life while
   it lasts.
Happiness is serving God – doing what's right –
   in the heart having a song;
Material assets never have and never will make
   happiness, secure and fast!
Happiness based only on outward circumstances –
   short-lived – and wrong!

Suspense

Suspense ... anxiety – that's something to measure your
    faith from,
Faith is the substance of things hoped for –
    the evidence of things not seen.
Suspense is mental uncertainty ...
    excitement to an outcome.
Books are written exciting many,
    and deemed –
Just a story with characters the author
    manipulates everyone ...
In life, things are for real ... more
    suspense with realities' sealed.
The actions of one ... many times as
    much danger as a gun.
Faith evens out the keel ... the Lord
    does support and heal.

Life is full of decisions all have to
    make.
Suspense or anxiety can be replaced
    by faith.
As we pray to the Lord for help ... who are
    we to say ... the path we take.
When God offers help through providential
    leading ... if refused, a lot is at stake.
Do we want help or determined to do
    things our own way ... a price we'll pay.
If we pray – "Lord, Thy Will be done" – then don't
    obey ... a mistake we make.
God sends help, but He chooses His own
    way.
We need pay attention to the answer He sends –
    our own judgment – suspend.

Why ask help at the start ... if we know
    best ... do what we may!
The Lord doesn't need our help to devise His
    choice of help ...
Remember He knows all about us – all the
    fears and doubts.

When we were small ... with a trusted parent
    even in danger, we'd just nap.
No anxiety or suspense – we felt safe ...
    not knowing what it was all about.
When God is in charge and we ask Him
    in faith ... He isn't obligated to draw us a map.
He sees all ... around each curve and bend ...
    one thing we can know, help He will send.
We did pray, on our knees did stay – the way man
    thinks – and God's better way ... a big gap.

What's the use beseeching the Lord for help when –
    your own decision is your reward ...
He'll work things out ... for your good
    He won't be dictated to ... neither He should.
After all, He is All-Powerful – we are the ones
    who need His regard.

Common To All

Do you have troubles ... heartaches and such?
Do you ... have aches and pains ... from head to heel?
Some days do you do better ... not hurting so much?
Do circumstances play a major role ... in how you feel?

These things are universal ... common to man ...;
Yet, each surmises – when trouble arises –;
That no one has ever suffered such trouble, as now at hand;
To forget reality ... how adversity comes to all isn't the wisest.

The Bible says, "Man born of woman is few days and full of
     trouble;"
Also, "Man is born unto trouble as sparks fly upward...;"
Without help and care of the Lord, man is as broken rubble –;
Reaching from land to sea ... heartaches, pain and trouble ...
     every continent marred.

Living Now

So many say…"Everything has gone wrong …;"
Yet, … just think – not all that could have gone –;
Even in the heartache that is today …
Happenings so much worse at our door could lay.
When we're prone to complain and say –,
All things have gone awry … but, nay …;
Not nearly so much as will and could be;
If we live longer … in time we'll be made to see.
Then to be in the condition … as we are now;
We would never complain again … a vow!

Thankfulness is always much in order;
Our great God fills our lives with manifold blessings to the
    border.
When we're thinking discouraging thoughts;
Count your blessings … not to become overly fraught.
Always look around you; many in worse condition;
Many are the plights to assay you, causing a heart's rendition.
Try looking beyond self to another's need …;
Helping assuage their misery … by word and deed.
The way to do service for the Lord is through humanity;
So with humble – thankful heart, at the foot of the cross, lay
    vanity.

Distance With God is Negligible

Dear friends ... we'll call you that – although – it's
   much more –.
In church capacity ... there is a spiritual bond of –
   closeness ...
Because in Salvation – we all recognize Christ as the
   One and only door ...;
To reach our Heavenly home with all its – celestial
   beauty and vastness.

While here on earth – there are times when one needs,
   must move ...
So thankful we should be ... that God is everywhere the
   same –.
Staying close to our Saviour – is the means of closeness
   to another – love will prove;
Separations come ... each person must fulfill their part –
   that's life – no one to blame.

Prayers can be heard ... no matter how far removed in miles –
   it really doesn't matter.
A closeness of spirits – it's the hearts that bind – love
   transcends – whatever the distance ...
So – in prayer remember us – as we'll remember you – one
   day all God's children – will all be together.
Pray God's will be done – be strong – trusting, believing –
   in Christian love, not restraint.

May our Great and Wonderful God – all-knowing – bless all
    of you, is our sincere prayer;
May He lead in helping find your place – in His service
    as you leave family and old friends;
You'll find – as we've found – many times in days gone by –
    loved ones and new friends make burdens easier to bear.
The Lord has made a way – even in times of trouble to have
    peace – faith always the base.

Too Busy

We can get so busy trying to run God's exclusive
    business –;
We either forget or refuse to do the work He has
    left us to do ...;
Thinking we know better than He ... doubting – we
    need confess;
Instead of doing His bidding ... our very own way
    we do pursue.

God's business is His own ... no explanation does
    He to anyone owe ...;
For what He does or doesn't do ... not consulting
    with man in lieu –;
Man has the Bible, God's word, to tell what we
    should know;
God's plan for man is in His Book ... for man to
    study ... then with his part to follow through.

When we turn away from God ... setting ourselves up
    to try and do His job ...;
We're exalting self as did the devil in the
    beginning ... as we know time –;
When in the garden of Eden ... he said he'd be like
    the most high God;
Following God's plan for the work of man is best ...
    we find.

Leaving God's business to Him ... is what we should ...
　　forever do ...;
Always seeking God's help in doing His work ... and
　　willing to do His bidding --;
Never so busy working ...we forget to worship ... souls
　　will be saved when we obey what's required of me and you.
No great thing to humble ourselves before a Great God ...
　　who upon His throne in Heaven is sitting ... pride in
　　　hearts ridding.

What's Next?

When trouble comes – what's next comes to
    mind ...
Searching this way and that – when a way
    out you can't find.
Such turmoil ... great trouble is with
    anguish to bind;
One cannot ... to despair ever be
    resigned.
Faith sees the way ... in the darkest
    of days.
Our eyes cannot see ... but our spirit
    may.

Strength comes from Christ – in Him it
    will always lay.
God leading ... mattering not "what is next"
    directing our path – ALL the way.
It matter not what others ... do ...
    or say ...
The devil can only do what God allows
    in hindering or delay –;
Vengeance is mine saith the Lord, "I
    will repay..."
So it behooves all who would do wickedly
    to answer the devil, "Nay!"

Understanding

… Do you ever lament the fact you're
   so misunderstood?
You meant to do or say it differently …
   didn't say what you would.
Feeling so badly – you would change the
   bad impression if you could …
If people could only understand … you
   meant it all for good.

Do you ever think others are vulnerable –
   perhaps, even more than you?:
Their hearts may be sorely tried, from
   being wrongly accused.
Bodies tired and worn … spirits ebbing
   sad and bruised …
Perhaps, an understanding spirit for them …
   the same as you – would great wonders do …

So …when you begin to think … you alone
   need understanding –;
Look about you … taking note of those –
   not so remote …
Who need your prayers – understanding,
   love and support –
Instead of only thinking of self – try a little
   understanding – thoughts of self, abandoning.

Smooth Sailing In The Storm

Everyone has disappointments ... frustrations
   and discouragements;
But, to live above these ... smooth sailing on a higher
   plane –;
Comes by looking to the Lord ... in faith, as
   life's defense;
To carry smoothly over life's pitfalls ...
   as snow covers the country lane.

Serenity and calmness characterizes
   the Spirit ...
When resting in the security of God's
   love and power –;
Nothing can harm, but what a loving God
   allows ... one need not fear it;
Strength not our own ... but that
   of the Lord, our Tower.

Oh, what comfort we forfeit when in life's storm,
   drawing away from God ... shrinking further still –;
When God would have us draw
   nearer ... His words to hear –;
In repentance and faith ... in love
   to seek His all-knowing Will;
His strength upholds ... carrying safely
   and securely over the storm without fear.

Love Hides

The Bible tells us ... love hides a multitude of
    sins ...;
Overlooking what's considered another's fault
    speaks well of you;
We're not to compromise the truth ... but, stand
    for right, in our compassion –;
While with wisdom and understanding we grant to
    all, the dignity's that's due.

Love never vaunts itself ... or behaves itself
    unseemly ... at another's expense;
To validate how intelligent one may be ...
    mattering not – no wisdom is spent;
Love never casts down with nothing constructive
    for action ... hence ...;
Love doesn't resent another's accomplishments ...
    perhaps, to you not lent.

Hiding a multitude of sins ... means overlooking
    ... not stirring up strife –;
To love ... is to always have the benefit of the
    other in mind ...;
Criticism that isn't constructive ... everywhere
    is rife;
Yet, hearts that love and care ... crosses of
    another will bear – for love does bind.

Before and After

Sunshine is so very nice ... so warm and
    especially bright – just after storm-clouds and rain;
With sun all the time ... there'd be much
    dust – you would find –;
Would be so hot ... sun scorching the lot ...
    and of heat all would complain ...
In the absence of the sun ... then when again
    the shining has begun – for awhile heat isn't brought to mind

The same can be said ... in the living
    of our lives –;
If all things were exactly as we thought
    and sought ... wanting for naught;
How ineffective life without adversity ...
    would be ...
After some trouble or hardship has drawn us
    close to the Lord – more willing are we to obey as we ought.

We should never expect all things in life to go smoothly.
We're not to always look for the easy way out –;
When decisions must be made – affecting
    others – not only thee or me;
Best stay on the right route ... and God's
    instructions – not doubt ...
For plainly in God's Word – is written God's
    plan ... for everyone to see.

In a Nutshell

The Bible tells us … to love our neighbor as
    ourselves …;
Also, not to think of ourselves more highly
    than we ought –;
So many lives are left … giving or receiving
    of love bereft;
If loving … as by our Lord we're taught … what
    changes we'd see wrought !!!

Slap Happy

He may be happy …,
But, he doesn't look happy!
He may be happy …;
Not looking happy!

That's why he looks so glum!
Because when he's happy;
You can't tell he's happy.
So … why be happy …?

When you don't look happy;
And no one knows you're happy,
… Maybe you aren't happy,
Though you thought you were happy!

If you thought you were happy;
Others didn't think you were happy,
… So why be happy …?
Just be glum … that's the sum!!

It's Your Life, So Say So!

Who could be so bold as to say ... "A life put on
   hold...,"
Life presses on – inching toward eternity each and
   everyday ... just life's way!
We need enjoy each day as we go ... not such
   regrets – to sit around ... to worry and fold!
Some of the things we plan to do ... have to wait –
   time passes on ... just a delay.
Sometimes it seems ... others take delight to,
   "pity" someone, who escaped their plight ...
"To each his own" a very wise statement – another's
   predicament – to you might seem as in bondage sold!

So what we make of life is up to us ... choices
   made – don't make lightly!
Each has his life's "row" to hoe – don't be taken in –
   best go slowly ... not quite so bold;
Asking God in decisions to be rendered ... if He
  comes first ... it has to be right!
If to God you have been true ... your life's, "on
   track" – whatever your goal – whatever you do!
When someone declares ... "Your life's on hold" –
   just say – I've escaped a lot of snares out of sight!"
If you enjoy your station in life – speak out –
   be as bold as they are bold – they need be told!

Which?

Is it we forget to remember ...;
Or in remembering ... choose to forget?
The affliction of so many ... as it were;
Oh, if only memory and forgetfulness ... quietly met!

Many happenings ... when remembered are glossed over;
Then, at times, the best included in ... forgetfulness is from
    memory wrest;
To say one, "ALWAYS" remembers the "FACTS" ... a
    misnomer.
Selective memory is "most fabulous" with MEMORY at its
    best.

Past experience is an excellent learning tool ...;
If reflection on the past ... we see our mistakes;
Much can be learned to correct – as a rule –;
God gives wisdom to those who ask and wait ... not
    acquired by fate.

Doctrinal and Didactic

The Powers That Be

We need understand … ordained of God are the powers …,
    that be;
There is no power but of God … He is able to restrain the
    one … allowing another to go free.
At times, God permits evil men to be exalted in power all
    will agree …;
They're allowed a time in place to fulfill God's plan for
    the human race.

God has the power … overrules and casts aside many things
    at His will …;
We must stand firm for Christ and right … while God's plan
    is fulfilled.
Daniel of old … though meek … his unwavering faith in God
    made him bold –;
Standing firm for what was right … his life and influence
    to the devil was never sold.

Daniel doing by faith that which was right … as opportunities
    came along;
Gained him great influence with King Nebuchadnezzar … so
    set to do wrong.
So limited is man in seeing and understanding a great God's
    plan –,
Who never needs or seeks advice … EVER from the likes of …
    man.

God allows many wicked to prosper – gain prestige and worldly
   fame …;
Realizing it or not … they're subject to a God who knows
   their blame –.
To bring His will to pass, God uses all: the righteous, the
   wicked, the weak and stout;
Everything written and prophesied in God's word will …
   certainly come about.

His Will

Man was created by God ... with a will ... the power
    of choice –;
God allows man to choose ... the choice is yours ...
    whether it be right or wrong ...
Man is God's creation; therefore, dependent ... but,
    man still has a choice;
The outcome of man's decision ... is made manifest
    in time ... be it short or long.

The winds and waves obeyed back then ... while here
    on earth He did command –;
The storm quieted when He spoke the quieting words –
    "Peace be still" ...
God created man with a will ... desiring him to choose
    right ... fulfilling a righteous God's demands.
God receives glory when man willingly chooses right,
    exalting God's will.

The wind and waves have no will of their own; therefore,
    ... no decision to make ...
When our Lord gave command for the storm to cease ...
    the wind and waves were still –;
Right choices should be made, praying God's will be
    done ... doing what we do for His sake ...;
Only one way to give glory to God ... as the wind and
    waves obeyed ... yield our will to His will.

To Forgive

To forgive, God's Word teaches we're to do ...
When someone asks our forgiveness,
Then God will not forgive you;
For God's blessings, we must forgive our sisters and brothers.

It seems, at times, it's easier to forgive others than self;
No one does everything without blight.
In one's self there's much to forgive;
Yet, trying, with God's help, always to do right.

One must forgive own failures ... while learning;
Never quit trying to improve in right ...
Self-forgiveness in acceptance and discerning;
Makes one's life more enjoyable and bright.

Holding a grudge against others is a sin;
Yet, how much we are stymied not forgiving as we do them;
All of us, at times, would like to do over what has been;
With faith in Christ, we must push forward, trusting Him.

What we're required to do for others, we should do for ourselves.
Forgiveness always makes the heart a more pleasant abode;
Of all the things others do against us is shelved,
Forgiving what we do detrimental to ourselves makes a
    lighter load.

God forgives us when we in repentance
    come to Him ...
If God forgives ... then we need move
    on with our lives –;
Not let the devil beat us down ...
    our faith growing dim;
Increased faith in the Lord ... does
    the devil defy.

Time Will Tell

Much time may elapse from an offense to
    reckoning ... quite a distance;
For God is long-suffering ... not willing
    that any should perish;
But, that all should come to repentance –
    yielding to His Spirit – not resistance ...
Though our sins be as scarlet ... they shall
    be as white as snow – white not garish.

When we suffer wrong ... from doing and
    standing for right;
"Vengeance is mine," saith the Lord, "I will
    repay."
God is keeping record ... and holds accountable –
    in His light.
Let there be no retaliation – have faith in
    God to bring to justice ... though a delay.

It is better to suffer wrong than
    to be a wrongdoer;
For a good conscience ... to abundant
    living is necessary and dear –;
Ordeals of suffering seem to increase –
    not be fewer.
Born in sin, we can't escape all effects
    of evil – God is the One all need to fear.

God is able to cast both body and soul
    into Hell;
Yet, He offers Salvation ... through the
    Sacrificial death of Jesus, His Son –;
Eternity isn't just ... for a short space ...
    or spell ...
It's either Heaven or Hell ... eternity is
    as a circle – without an ending – none.

Strength in Weakness

The devil beats and hammers on us each
    day;
In our weakest moments, daring to see if
    he can sway –.
We need to pray and study even more –
    telling him, "Nay!"

Faith can move mountains, keeping the
    devil – at bay.
The strength of God's Hand holding … ,
    making him stay!
Staying close to our Lord … if we desire
    to, we may.
With broken spirit and contrite heart, to
    His will answer, "Yea."

The devil is a liar and father of lies –
    nothing good to say.
Desiring to lead all humanity to hell and
    the – depths of decay.
Failing to accept Christ as Saviour – in
    hell, you'll pay.
God gave His Son – Christ gave His life,
    to take our sin away!

Waiting ... Just For You!

In the Seventh Chapter of Proverbs ... about a
    young man void of understanding – we're told;
A woman with the attire of an harlot ... in the
    street, at every corner – waiting so bold;
The Scripture says ... she comes to meet – for you
    she seeks ... on every corner and in the street.
No one needs to feel flattered ... but, please take note,
    anyone she'll greet ... she happens to meet ...
Truth is, it doesn't matter to her ... who comes
    along –;
Waiting in the street and on the corner ... for
    just ANYONE ... she can entice to do wrong.

When straying from the path that's right ... sins
    do mount ...when judgment's not sound –;
With a multitude of homes broken up ... many lives
    ruined – turned upside down ...
Forgiveness and Salvation are through Christ ...
    else there is none;
But, the sordid behavior can never be forgotten
    or deeds undone.
When the Bible says a, "reproach" that will ...
    NEVER leave you ... it never can;
A life of faith and obedience ... meeting the ...
    approval of God – uplifts a woman or man.

Anyone You Know?

The Bible says ... rebellion is as the sin of witchcraft, stubbornness is as iniquity and idolatry;
Do you or anyone you know ... always have to have
their own say?
A person can be so obsessed with self – whether right
or wrong ... stubbornness is from an age of antiquity;
When, "me, myself and I" are paramount ... idolatry not
at bay – idolizing self ... another way to say.

Stubbornness and rebellion are not the fruits of a
Godly spirit ...;
Meekness, temperance, kindness, faith, purity and truth
are attributes to seek after;
One should seek to be rid of stubbornness and rebellion –
with God's help, through prayers, abhor and fear it;
In Salvation, a new heart is given ... afterwards, obedience
to God – the main factor.

When a person prays ... then sincerely ends with, "Thy
Will, not mine be done" and from the heart ...;
Stubbornness and rebellion are left to the devil –
making no headway in recognizing the evil;
Then, the sin of idolatry and witchcraft have no part,
yet, an age-old tool is the devil's mart.
Never fail in standing for truth and right ... being
grounded in the faith ... regardless of upheaval.

Way Back When

Do you remember ... when, "pardon me" meant – perhaps some
    minor offense as bumping with an elbow ...;
Stepping on a toe ... reaching in front of – just small
    things ... as they go –
Now, " pardon me" ... calls to mind Presidential pardons,
    so many ... looking to find;
When the tangle is such ... it not yet hushed ... the one
    with the pardons ... could rush from behind.

Do you remember ... when killing someone meant ... though
    by different degrees ... murder;
Penalties were decreed by our Courts – from jail time to
    the death sentence, so crime was deterred further ...;
For years now, we've had a (doctor?) ... referred to by
    many as Dr. Death!
Something to contemplate ... will he be so anxious to meet
    His Maker, the giver of life, as he draws his last breath?

Do you remember ... when in marriage it wasn't hard to tell
    who was the husband and who the wife ...
As God in the Garden of Eden ... gave Eve to Adam and he
    called her, "woman" ... to be his for life;
Now Congress spends our tax money and their "elected"
    time ... judging what constitutes a marriage –;
Illicit same sex relationships ... in God's Word is condemned
    ... utterly disparaged.

Do you remember when ... abortion was considered sinful ...
though, " unsuccessfully" so, desired to remain secret ...;
Sin is sin, now as then ... seeking to make it discreet – judges
and congress ... to legalize it do meet;
God is everywhere ... He sees all, knows all ... knows the
exact time of the stopping the least heartbeat.
No one will be able to "twist" God's law around the Great
White Throne Judgment, or Christ's Judgment Seat.

Our Founding Fathers had none of these conditions to grapple
with in forging the Constitution, they had in mind.;
When they served their country under hardships ... with the
good of the people, in the standard of laws they did define.
They loved God and country ... and knew they were elected to,
"serve" ... "Government of the people, by the people and for
the people" ...
Their laws were modeled after God's Law, in the Bible ...
God's Law with no flaw ... nothing degrading or feeble.

Why Should There Be a Question?

Why should there be any doubt …
As to what constitutes a marriage?
The Bible tells us plainly what marriage is about.
Anything less than God's plan is … by man rearranged.

Never can be made void the Scriptures which say …
A man shall leave his father and mother and cleave to his wife;
Also, man is to honor his wife as the weaker vessel … not may;
A wife is to see she reverence her husband - in life.

One man … one woman, is God's plan – not to go by fashion;
For the purpose of procreation of the human race …;
It has been said, "The home is the backbone of a nation":
God's Word will stand … man disobeys, but never can efface.

If man could have complete control over all!!!!
With some to proclaim … a marriage of two … sex the same –
Such baseness is an abomination … the Bible proclaims;
What a disaster to so little value life as one, "base" game.

Between two of the same sex … a marriage it isn't …;
Even the animal kingdom have better instincts …even rats –
Some animals and fowls pair for life … with the opposite sex;
In the higher order of creation … God expects better than that.

It has been said . "When two of the same sex make eyes at
each other; two "nerds" have met … "going in the same
      direction …:"
God's Word strongly condemns all this as lust, they call love;
God is love; anything contrary to His teaching cannot be love …
      warrants no retraction.

Values Instilled

A mother has great responsibility when
   raising a son ...
Since you are his example ... you may
   be, he'll take his actions from –;
In raising children ...we no doubt will
   all see the proof later on of what we've done.
The proof of the pudding is exhibited – all
   people aren't so dumb!

He may become president or maybe a lawyer
   who defends –
But, one thing for sure – a mother will answer
   to God for values she ran away from –
If a mother spends her time hanging out at
   "hell holes" and gambling dens ...
Race tracks and such – how should one expect
  anything of Christian values from her son.

When it comes time for God to give out rewards
   for service done –;
It will be mother who lived right and took
   her direction from God's Word.
Not a mother who had no moral values and
   taught her son none –
Rewards in heaven will be handed out – to those
   who are saved and God's Word heard.

It matters not the race or physical
   stature ...
The complexion or color of hair – if it's
   two colors or one ...
A mother as well as others need adhere to
   truth ... in the future.
After all, worldly "quirks of fame" won't
   stand when all is said and done !

Respecter of Persons

Are you a respecter of persons ... one of life's popular
    games?
God is no respecter of persons ... He states this
    in His word;
We know this is true – it's our attitude which makes
    the difference - all not the same.
God reacts to man ... in many instances ...
    as man reacts to God.
What God does is for our good ... He knows us
    all by name.
We are His creation ... He made us from
    the sod.
Though He is God over all ... yet, in rejection of
    Christ as Saviour – we must accept the blame.
Salvation is free – Christ died for you and me ...
    The Holy Spirit continues to prod.
No matter how it seems to us ... we can know –
    God in His judgment – is always true.
What about man's way of doing things ... is
    to do right ... the measuring rod?

Do we have respect of persons ... in this life –
    there are many who dare
In as much as possible ... do we give treatment
    considered fair? ... something untrue ...
If you're telling, do you choose someone
    who loves and is lenient with you
Rather than someone who you personally ... mean nothing
    to them only the truth.
Yet ... your own loved ones' feelings ... are so
    easily cast aside;
When the hurt rendered there ... is many times –
    as with a knife – hearts laid bare.

Our first obligation is to God – to do right – then
    to the family in which we reside.
Not just for show ... to those who many times –
    don't even care or want to know;
If one desires a peaceful life ... respect all ...
    but, especially family – your husband or wife.
They are the ones – always hurt the most ...
Remember – you'll reap whatsoever you sow!!

Determination is Rife!

In the Bible – in the Book of Ruth – remember
    Naomi's daughter-in-law … Ruth?
To Naomi – Ruth was a true friend – ready to
    share the hardships Naomi saw.
In Genesis … we read of another instance …
    the very opposite – of a truth.
Rebekah and Isaac were sorely troubled about
    their daughter-in-law;
At the end of Chapter twenty-seven – in the
    book of Genesis – to despair reduced!
Esau took to wife of the daughters of Heth in
    the land of Canaan;
He was forty years old … should have had better
    judgment – not easily seduced!
Rebekah said to Isaac – "I'm weary of my life,
    because of the daughters of Heth."

Esau's marriage was a grief of mind to Isaac
    and Rebekah; in reading, it's easy to see.
If Jacob, the other son – takes a wife such as
    these, which are of the daughters of the land;
Rebekah lamented to Isaac … " What good shall my
    life do me?"
Isaac blessed Jacob – gave him a charge – sent him
    away … following their plan …;
They sent him from Canaan to Padan-Aran … to his
    Mother's father, Bethuel,
To find a wife in a different land – where lived
    his kin – they didn't ban.
Isaac and Rebekah sent Jacob away … they were
    adamant in their refusal.
As parents, they saw the need of taking a stand …
    their attitude –"do what we can!"

Rebekah and Isaac with legitimate concern – for
  Jacob – sent him with relatives to stay;
Though he didn't marry of the daughters of the
  Land of Canaan,
His uncle Laban tricked him concerning the wife he
  chose … twice he did pay.
Leah was his wife – Rachael, he had to pay double to
  make her his wife – working as he could.
When they were moving, Rachel took her "false gods"
  when they left – on the camel they lay.
It mattered not how faraway Jacob went … God was
  over all the land.
God, at times, overrides situations to work His Will –
  Jacob was father of Israel's twelve tribes.
The name "Jacob" means trickster –it seems left to
  himself – he was headlong once and again!

What type of daughter-in-law would you make or –
  choose …;
Ruth or the daughters of Heth, of the land of
  Canaan?
Daughter-in-laws have a choice as to what they …
  will do.
As a daughter-in-law … do you serve God or
  mammon?
You can have the attributes of Naomi's daughter –
  in-law, Ruth … it's up to you;
Or be like the daughter of Heth of the land of
  Canaan – spirit like that of Haman.
If yielding our lives to the will of Christ … and
  right, we pursue – we'll be as Ruth …
A blessing to Mother and Father-in-law, yea, to
  all … when selfishness turns to love!

Digging Out, or By Faith?

Are you burdened down with heartache in life ...
Buried deep beneath a mountainous load of care –;
Have others caused much heartbreak and strife?
Adding to your burdens ... more they expect you to bear.

Wherever you go, you'll always find God in force to be there;
Giving help to His own ... through Christ the Lord –;
When one asks ... in faith – the Lord always gives help and
    care.
Faith ... though unseen has evidence of reward.

Faith raises one from the deep miry pit to a higher plain;
Clearing life's rubble ... pushing out of the way.
Sunlight of God's love with blessings, eases the strain.
By faith, you anticipate, though not yet seeing a brighter day.

Not digging out by the arms of the flesh, mountains moved by faith;
Flying with wings to the Lord ... faith's Haven of Rest.
"Vengeance is mine, saith the Lord ... I will repay ...;"
We need pray – letting retaliation ... stay, anything other is
    less than our best.

A Serious Matter

Marriage and divorce are serious steps to
   take.
Best to try a new start with the –
   old,
Than make with someone new, the same old
   mistake.
Old for new can become an unsavory –
   roll, a great number fit the mold!

If it's only bickering over money, in-laws and
   such;
Repent – turn to God for help – through a Loving
   Christ.
Some interest, working together – resolving –
   much.
Be honest, sincere and true, heart to heart –
   no lies.
      considerate – not pious!

It's better to try – with the old – a new
   start ...;
Than to make an – old start – with someone
   new.
If continuing, to play at life – in the same
   roll and part;
Multiple divorces ... are the poll ... there's your
   cue! Straighten up – in lieu!

There are situations when only one is at
    fault.
If one to the other proves base and –
    untrue;
Even God allows the wronged one to bring the hurt
    to a halt.
Dissolving the marriage … though their best they
    did do.
       without guilt – life to pursue!

When married, if each loves the other as they
    should,
With God's help, trying and remembering, the –
    reason why.
Forgiving – things can change – with God's help
    they would.
What, married again? To one say, "Bye" … so soon
    to another, "Hi"!
       many regret – until they die!

The Outward and the Inward Man
(II Cor. 4:16)

While the outward man is perishing,
The inward man's renewed day by day;
Each year, more signs of aging are seen,
Only death will hold old age at bay.

Growing feeble with steps uncertain,
Eyes dim ... wrinkles line the once firm face;
Strength fails ... small things become such burdens;
Thinking what might have been ... without grace.

While energy did abound for years,
Time moved swiftly – even years passed fast;
So much leisure days seem endless
Aches and pains can in the doldrums cast.

A body once strong, now just creeps along,
Weakness takes over where strength has been;
Such effort to answer dinner's gong,
Adam's fall plunged us all into sin.

Through Christ ...the inward man's made alive
God's great Salvation brings peace sublime,
When we're saved, living for Christ we strive,
Rejoice in the inward man ... for renewed ... cannot die.

But, all the discomfort of old age,
Can't compared with what's to come later,
In Heaven, there'll be none of sin's wage,
War of flesh and inward man won't rage.

The Wicked

The wicked flee – the Bible tells us – when
    no man pursueth …
A person's guilt – though kept inside
    causes one to quake …
Fear and guilt … aren't compatible
    with valor and courage – it escheweth –.
Guilt and wickedness cause a person to be
    a coward – courage can't be fake.

The wicked fleeing when no man pursueth
    will cause much confusion …
God can and has caused those on
    the same side to fight as foes –;
In Biblical times, God has done this very
    thing – causing His enemies to see illusions.
"The righteous are as bold as lions …" is the
    way the word of God goes.

Talk about confusion and its most agonizing
    turmoil and sure defeat …
The wicked turning this way and that – running
    over themselves to break free –
Someday, our Lord will give victory and call a halt to
    everything to do with deceit and retreat …
For when our Great God intervenes, He'll disrupt all
    the wicked and malicious plans He sees.

Child Abuse

Child abuse is something much abhorred
    and much cried ... out about.
Abuse before birth – is of another sort ... causing
    much pain and much at risk –.
Before and after a baby is born ... so many legitimate
    doubts ...
Many things can harm a baby ... before
    birth as well as after – take care –is the gist.

Before a baby's entrance is made into
    a world – confusing and filled with pain ...
Many things – in not taking care – stems from
    monetary gain and greed –;
A tiny baby not yet born ... should
    have rights ... the mother's body is his domain...
His livelihood and food ... depend upon the
    other – his only way to feed.

When a mother uses cocaine ... the baby
    is abused ...
Coming into the world ... with a need
    for drugs – is fused –;
But, what about the woman who chooses not to
    rest – doesn't eat right on some mythical ruse.
Never makes any allowance concerning changes
    the baby requires – that's abuse.

A balanced diet … foods a varied … colorful
   riot …
To give the babe a chance see what
   food it likes –
Child abuse is to be shunned – to be
   stopped – before it's begun …
That means after the baby is born or while
   still in the womb.

A child's health later on … can not be
   separated from care before it was born –;
Doing the best that can be done – trusting
   the Lord about our daughter or son …
Praying should always be done –
But, the Lord doesn't do what the mother should have
   done.
If a woman is unconcerned about the baby … better she
   remained as was and never had one.

They're Precious To Some

Precious are children ... to all they should be,
The Lord said, "Suffer little children, to come unto me ."
Tiny and helpless, dependent – therefore, to some no rights at
    all;
God remembers the little children – it might help, to recall.
Without His knowledge ... not one sparrow does fall.
Yet, the unborn are mistreated so – does really appall.

A thousand miles away – a baby expected any day ...;
A phone call in the night – to our hearts dear;
First thing we ask ..."Is she alright ..."
Is everything there as it should be? ... turning on the light.
A moment while we listen – hearts full of care;
So sleepy – yet ... thanking God for answered prayers.

Grandparents aren't just by-standers or shouldn't be –;
The baby that is born is yours – a part of them you see.
When they cared for you many years, as best they could,
Sometimes, in very harsh circumstances, together they stood.
Best to cultivate patience – no high-horse will work;
For you know their love, in the background will always lurk.

Oh, the new baby – so good, to have and so fine;
So proud – the same as you – love – hearts do bind.
You are the concern of your parents' love ...;
Always praying – God give His help from above,
The baby expected or born to you ...;
Is of its ancestors ... and not a few.

Be thankful to God for blessings received –;
Not any deserve ... what He gives so freely ...
Whatever we have ... or might ever be,
Is unmerited favor ... be not deceived;
Turning to God ... always asking for grace ...
Teach the child right ... Christ is the base.

God is So Good

God is so good … to each and all …;
So much … our thoughts are limited;
We see not the full scope – to recall.
So many blessings He gives – heartaches remedied.

Joy to a home … through a baby loaned,
Beautiful little face – eyes shining like stars;
Little hands and feet – a perfect little body, donned.
Though commonplace – each birth a miracle –

God blesses, with children added to a home;
Teaching them right – as they grow along …
Giving something back … for one not our own;
We just have them for a space in time, to God they belong.

Train up a child in the way it should go …
The way of salvation – always make plain –
Honoring God … for the blessing He did bestow;
For there's Hell to shun and a Heaven to gain.

God will help through the years ahead …;
Ask those older … who many times have said …
Trusting God for help … by His spirit led …
How to raise a family … in God's word – "it can all be read."

New Voices

New voices old as the devil himself – Truth doesn't
   change!
Though Truth seldom leads to the road of fame.
Heed the direction in life you take –.
It makes a great difference – make no mistake!
Truth is paramount – even to living in a hovel.
So stand up straight … not fearful and grovel!

New voices are heard … many our deadly foe!
Do not succumb … or kowtow!
Our Lord's the only One we're to bow to …
He's the only One! - everything He does benefits you.
If to Him you belong … He'll correct as a son.
Chastisement's never pleasant – if it were – leave undone!

New voices will deceive – we're not to adhere to;
If foreign to the Truth – they'll just never do!
We're told in the Bible, "Study to show ourselves approved
Unto God, a workman that needeth not to be ashamed,
… rightly dividing the Word of Truth …!"
Studying as we should – Truth will never seem uncouth!

Emotions?
Or
Grow Up!

Emotions ... intense feelings as of love,
    hate or despair ...
A person whose life is ruled only by
    emotions ...;
Is someone to be pitied ... yet, to be
    around is hard to bear;
To deal with such ... if you've never
    done much – you simply have no notion.

Tears ... flow at every provocation and
    where there is none;
Always searching for something they
    can hate or dislike –;
The crying starts ... eyes flowing to the
    brim – salty tears – do run;
'Till one thinks ... somewhere out of sight –
    there has to be a faulty dyke!

After getting their way ... the tears dry up –
    soon dry as a desert –;
They got the attention ... it's the way
    they work –;
Reminds you of a child throwing a
    tantrum – going bezerk –.
When not getting their way ... they
    begin to kick and jerk.

Emotions of love – hate and despair,
  along with others …
Have their part in the lives of all –
  but, have their place;
They need to grow up take – their place
  in life … husbands are not their mothers.
If you're to have a family – your own …
  better do some thinking – asking God's grace.

Many divorces could be avoided if both
  desire … to see what's lacking …;
Want to get married … then when
  hardships come – the tantrums begin –;
Not long until the one trying to do right
  gets worn out – soon one is packing …
If tears, hate and love are only based on
  emotion … all this to the turmoil does lend.

Don't be a juvenile … all your livelong
  life …
Responsibility in adults … seems to be
  so lacking –;
Many want to be as the children … desiring
  to exchange roles with offspring is rife –;
All this adds up – to just one thing –
  selfishness – and of immaturity backing.

Parents, let children be the children … they'll soon grow
  in life … don't let emotions exclude good thinking.
What a pitiful sight … and such a
  plight …
One finds one's self … bogged down with
  fantasy – linking –;
For each is responsible for – hardships
  to share – life, at times, is hard for all to bear.

Thankless

"As thankless as a toothless child:" … Scripture
   referring to a baby – teaching you and me;
A baby, so lovable, helpless, dependent, demanding,
   thankless … everything for granted – all for free.
Do we, as we grow into adulthood continue to feel
   the same … as if life's only a game;
When we're old and grey, still accepting all God's
   blessings without being thankful – we're to blame.
Take a look around … so many benefits furnished by
   God … what is there to be, "thankless" about?!
Many priceless blessings are bestowed upon saint as
   well as sinner … no doubt.

Much taken for granted, by everyone … air we breathe,
   flowers, trees, water, sunshine as well as the rain;
Just a few to name … for the just and unjust benefiting
   the same …;
Shameful to neglect thankfulness … toward a God who
   loves us so …
He gave Jesus, His Son, for the Salvation of our soul –
   yet, we treat Him not as a loving Father, but as a foe.
To be as, "thankless a toothless child" … means
   ingratitude … life wlll soon be gone …;
If one has teeth … perhaps the one's now are not your
   own – thank you to the Lord is due, and best, by actions
     shown.

It is Your Life

Envying and strife are not attributes of the Spirit
of God ...
The Bible says ... where they exist there is confusion
and every evil work –;
Every evil work ... covers all the evil the devil does
with us prod .
Wherever we fail – the devil does lurk – gloating ...
that obedience to God we again did shirk.

When godliness permeates a life, envying and strife are
not characteristic flaws.
The fruit of the Spirit is ... love, joy, peace, long-
suffering, gentleness ...
Goodness, faith, meekness, temperance ... against such
there is no law."
Christ came that we might have life and have it more
abundantly ... evil – a Godly Spirit does resist.

"My grace is sufficient" ... saith the Lord – where more
grace is needed, more grace is given to man.
We're told in God's word ... draw nigh unto God, and He
will draw nigh unto you ...
We're admonished to ... "Resist the devil and he will
flee from you," ... this promise covers the land.
Humble yourselves in the sight of the Lord, and He shall
lift you up ... if this you do.

Seeing Through It All

What may appear as excellent to some ...;
Not so to others ... judged from a different view –;
Words so easily put together ... yet, when done;
Words that deeds eschew ... speaking louder to all of us.

Do actions, public ... make for a different choice ...;
Do deeds perceived hidden ... if known – accolades would
    destroy;
What seems to be and what really is ... speak with a different
    voice,
No peace without Christ ... life with a deadly mixture of sin's
    alloy.

God looks into our hearts ...;
To the world what may seem hidden ... but, what is true there.
Does conviction for right ... strike as do darts;
The façade of words tumble ... motives laid bare.

The adage, "actions speak louder than words" ... shines
    bright;
As true today ... although stated so long ago ...;
God has made a way when we do wrong ... to do right;
Repentance ... asking forgiveness through Christ makes this
    so.

We can fool ALL the people SOME of the time ...;
All need learn this lesson and learn it well –;
We can fool SOME of the people ALL of the time;
But, we can't fool God ANY of the time ... He holds the keys
    to Hell.

Real Comfort

Best adhere to the things you know …
Don't be led astray because, of some saying so –;
Never change your beliefs just to seem smart;
Or in something untrue you'll likely take part.

Whatever the Bible states will come to pass …
At the end of time … many will be aghast –;
God's Word is always the basis;
In obeying it … our life can be an oasis.

Put no confidence in the flesh …
But, when trusting the Lord … heart and spirit will mesh;
Christ, the Saviour is the rock of our Salvation –
All manmade plans we're to shun, no benefit to anyone.

Rejecting Christ as Saviour … leaves only Hell …
Those refusing … in the judgment all will not be well;
The power of choice God gives to man –
Matters not where one may dwell throughout the land.

According to the Scriptures, time for man is running out;
If you don't believe it … study will do away with doubt.
God gave His only begotten Son, the sacrifice for sin …
Christ stood as a Lamb slain … before time began.

Thankfulness to God for His wonderful gift …
Should always be remembered … giving hearts a lift.
In the midst of troubles, peace will forever stay –
For our Lord is always there … pointing the way.

Such comfort … real comfort, in knowing Christ as Saviour;
Trusting and believing in God's Son … nothing good we've done;
The Bible tells us … He always cares for His own …
There's security for the believer in knowing if we're His,
 Heaven's our home.

Not Seeing Right!

Do you invariably go by outward appearance?
Not caring the condition inside ...
Could be many blessings and opportunities missed;
Because of your assistance denied.

Isaiah, chapter fifty-three tells of Christ's passion ...
At His coming ... when we shall see Him–
Christ hath no form or comeliness ...
There is no beauty that we should desire Him.

Though Christ has no outward beauty to look upon;
He's the only one who ever lived on earth a perfect life.
Christ was God manifest in the flesh; humanity's cloak He donned.
He gave Himself on Calvary's Cross ... His blood, Salvation's
    price.

When man thinks more highly of himself than he ought ...
God knows how to humble ... His timing just right –;
If we're to serve the Lord, His will, not another's should be sought.
We're not our own; He provided the sacrifice ... He paid the price.

The place Christ was born was a manger ... very small ...
Yet, He was the only begotten Son of God –;
Never judge by outward appearance when God gives His service
    call;
Who are we to reject and condemn by what we see; we're only of
    the sod.

The Lord's church is not the building …
Whether a great modern structure or an unappealing place;
Does the doctrine taught of the Spirit and truth ring?
Is truth's clarion call of grace to lost souls the base?

God may have a work waiting for you …
Hearing the Word, many souls … will come to Christ for
    Salvation;
Exalted thoughts … putting us above our Master, always
    eschew –
When life is done … those saved will be judged by God's own Son.

The Lord's church is to be a place of worship …
Neither the pastor nor friends should ever be the exalted ones;
Adhering to God's truths … standing for right … before
    fellowship –;
Paramount in church should be to worship in Spirit and truth …
    God, and Christ, His Son.

Prevention

God's word teaches we're to discipline our children;
We're taught to correct ... so their ways they'll mend -
"Spare the rod and spoil the child" -;
Chastening isn't in God's sight ... considered vile.

The Scripture does say ... God chastens His own ...;
If we be without chastisement ... to God we don't belong.
God knows just how to chasten ... to benefit us best -;
Prevents our straying further ... as on Him we turn to rest.

There's a lesson in the Bible for parents to learn.
It's because of "love," God desires right and wrong we discern;
Parents are accountable for how children are taught -;
Great responsibility for each child into the world that's brought.

A stitch in time... saves nine ...;
It's parent's duty to teach their children "to mind."
God expects no less from those He calls His own;
When in Salvation ... the name of "Christian" we don.

God's way is always the very best ...;
The government ... welfare ... instead of family's, a mess.
Prevention of crime ... best start in the heart -;
Mothers and dads ... in the home's the place to start.

Seasonal and Occasional

Nonstop or Time!

Thought I'd do a little writing ...
But, haven't had the time.
Thanksgiving and Christmas coming,
Work, with shopping combined.

To write a poem was heeded ...
What to write is needed –;
So many things come to remind;
Ways God has blessed defined.

Perhaps, there'll be a little space;
To slip away with grace ...
With pen and paper hidden out –;
Write a line ... there about.

One or two lines did come to me;
And profound ... were thought to be.
Before they could be written down;
Slipped from mind ... never found.

Many subjects to write about ...
FIRST ... thanks to God – no doubt;
Family with friends are brought to mind;
Feast set forth ...when we dine.

When company has come and gone ...
Holidays – passed along;
With house back to normal once more,
Writing won't be a chore.

Some do say, they like the last line;
At first, I thought it fine ...
On second thought, I knew what's meant –
Nothing subtle surrounds that HINT!

As the Old Year vanishes out ...
The New Year peeps on route;
My poem will be a little late,
Will have a New Year's date.

Though time to write is hard to find;
Those in jail have plenty time ...
They not only write, but dedicate –
To another, "wronged" ... jail mate.

With the tax money, mine and yours;
They're looked after for years,
Many have time to write a book ...
Turn famous in their, "nook."

It does seem crime is glorified …
Such attention they get –
While the rest search for time to rest;
Those doing, "Time" … have zest.

Writing when I get some time …
Words with value that rhyme –;
Looking to see if they're in print –
Spotting one from prison sent.

Oh well, must be politically correct;
Quota… in everything;
Just have to do the best I can …
Though free, yet, WORK demands.

Free … yet, do have obligations ….
To God and family, too.
While living with the rush of time;
Will try to rhyme a rhyme.

... King ...
From Manger to the Cross

Christmases come and go, love of it stays,
Nearing the time; all are counting the days;
Excitement mounts for everyone who's young,
While older hearts are with nostalgia wrung.

Remembering days that have gone before;
Some who were with us ... are with us no more;
Memories are precious when thinking back,
That left wanting, then – memory has no lack.

Christmas, celebrated as Jesus' birth ...
A time for thanksgiving, rejoicing, mirth;
Many things remind us all of Christmas:
Carol singing, lights and decorations;

Snow and ice ... baking with the smell of spice;
Shopping, greetings, eyes shining, smiles so nice;
Careful! Hustle and bustle ... doesn't stall ...
True meaning of Christmas, while hearts recall.

Gifts given to friends and family we love,
Greatest gift given came from God above:
He sent His own Son to die on the cross ...
For man in his sin was depraved and lost.

Christ ... God's sacrifice, willingly did die:
Man must repent, believe, renounce sin's pride;
Jesus, born in a manger, Saviour of man ...
Will be Lord of Lords, when He comes again.

Christmas means so much more than the world thinks,
More than tinsel and colored lights that blink;
A celebrated birth of the coming King ...
At His birth, the Heavenly Host, did sing.

Snow Flies

Winter is almost here … the snow will fly …
Icicles blowing in the wind, crack fine,
Snow covers ground where fall garden did lie;
So many good meals off which we will dine.

Holidays are always fun for family …
Feasting on meat, cakes, candy, cookies and pies …
No better food anywhere … all agree …
All anxiously await hot rolls to rise.

Popcorn for later … late or early snack …
One can hardly wait 'till snow flies in wind;
With big cups of coffee they all are back;
As limbs on big evergreens writhe and bend.

Gifts for all cover floor around the tree,
The excitement mounts as gifts are opened;
Fun is there for all … even old like me;
There's music and singing … you can depend.

Christmas is much more than what I write,
About Jesus, who on Christmas was born …
Nothing I can write more than Scriptures might,
All need accept Him and Saviour adorn.

The Big Snow

When the snow falls ever so thick
Certainly no one wants to be sick –
Such fun playing outside;
When others are by the fireside.
Coming in to get warm a bit;
No time to rest or sit.
Just get something hot to drink,
Then back to play – face still pink;
Finally with the snowman made;
Just before the sun did fade,
If it stays cold – he'll stand up bold,
If weather turns warm, he'll certainly fold.
But, whichever – we had such fun,
Building a snowman second to none;
Whether he stands or melts on the spot,
Or stays on and on – until it turns hot,
We had the most fun …we all do say,
Next year, when it snows – will be a "new day."

Christmas Season

The Christmas season's ... a joyous time;
Spicy potpourri – with evergreen –;
Among all the other aromas to find;
Filling the air ... everywhere it seems.

Tinkling of bells – music floating through the air;
  ... bringing back days of long ago ...
Remembering when young – enjoyment everywhere;
All things pertaining to Christmas – were enjoyed so.

If during the season – there should be snow;
Much the activities increased out-of-doors.;
Every hill, a gathering – all sleds in tow –;
Such laughter and singing as spirit's soar.

Snowflakes falling – snowballs flying through the air;
Choosing up sides ... playing at war;
Everyone snow-spattered ... not having a care;
Loosing mittens – caps coming off – heads all bare.

After the snow-filled battle – there's work to share;
Building a snowman – tall and stable ...
Lasting until the sun appears – and weather turns fair;
He'll melt so fast – taking the heat, he isn't able.

All that's left – where he stood so tall;
Is a puddle of water – with muddy slush ...
Cap, scarf, pipe and a few buttons is all;
Small children crying ... begging them to hush.

Explaining – the birth of Christ we celebrate;
Thanking God for His unspeakable gift to man;
Though history records, December 25th isn't the date –;
Yet, on this date, the birth of Christ – celebrated across the land.

What Gifts for Christ?

Christmas, to me, is winter's favorite time ...
    Christmas is almost here ...;
At Christ's birth, the Three Wise Men went to find –
    Jesus, the Babe, with hearts full of cheer –;
Desiring to see the Saviour ... to Bethlehem they
    did go; traveling far ... gifts they brought near.
Their love to the Saviour, they did show ... faith in
    God – lead by a star, turned away fear.

A desire for the Truth is pleasing to God we find ...
    after accepting Christ for the Salvation of our soul;
In repentance and faith, giving Him our heart for all
    time; come boldly to God's throne we're told.
Do we bring gifts to the One who loved us so ... on His
    birthday ... do we forget – leaving Him out ...
Shopping ... giving gifts to others wherever we go ...
    our hearts are what the Lord wants – no doubt.

God looks on the inside, not as others see ... a broken
    Spirit, and a broken and contrite heart, He does require;
Without faith, it's impossible to please Him ... and to
    please Him we should desire ...
Much we can do to show our love to the One who sent His
    only begotten Son to die for our sin ...
Sent the One so near His heart ... He came to us from
    above; to please the Lord with yielded life and heart ...
        each day repent ... no one is infallible ... repent.

Christmas

Christmas ... almost here ...
Another year ... gone;
What use have we been –
In the Master's work?
Christmas ever dear;
Loved ones coming home;
To us a Godsend ...
For love vanquishes hurt.

When Jesus was born ...
Babies killed ... Herod decreed;
Then, the same as now –
God worked His own plan;
Man should never scorn ...
He'll pay for all deeds;
In defeat he'll bow –
It's God's plan for man.

It's joy to the world;
Peace, goodwill, on earth;
As the Heavenly Host sang ...;
To announce His birth;
Glad tidings they herald;
Hosannas to His worth ...;
With joy the Heavens rang;
Felt, the whole world's girth.

Honor God ... living ...;
Give thanks for His Gift;
That from love did stem;
Was the best He had.
With Christmas giving ...
Our spirits do lift;
What do we give Him?
Forgetting ... so sad!!!

God is Love

Winter …
Cold … ice
Snowflakes,
Christmas,
Ribbons … bows
Gifts
Mince pies
Saviour
Born in manger
To save from sin.

"Bling."
Glitter,
Tinsel
On trees
What most see!
God so loved
From His heart
In Heaven
Jesus
Did rend.

Gifts

Gifts that come to me ...
Are the only ones to ever see –
None to buy, sew, or bake;
Nor none to give – just to take.

All the gifts under the tree;
Should be only for, "I, myself or me –;"
As contemplating on the gifts that be;
My name isn't on one gift – as I peek to see.

If choosing to have a part ...;
Must do some giving – making a start;
"It's better to give than to receive –;"
Sound farfetched to someone like me.

The Bible tells us better to give – is true;
To think of others is better in lieu;
For self always seeking to be first;
Usually we find ... one ends up worse.

What I Want For Christmas

What do I want for Christmas ... since I have my two front teeth?
   I'd like a tape recorder ...
A little, tiny, invisible one at that – that'll fit into purse
   or pocket ... just to order –;
Where people are gathered ... I can slip right in – no one need
   know ... being recorded ... perhaps, what is bad;
Being sneaky ... no one will ever guess just where I've been ...
   but, when played back ... they'll wish they had!!!

A tiny recorder would for the purpose work the best ... and a
   larger one will cost more dough ...
One can always do just like the rest ... carry a large purse
   and make big, big pockets in skirt or shirt when you sew.
It does mean this season recording is all the RAGE ... can't see
   to my job ... for reporting;
Some say there's hardly enough work done to earn my wage ...
   but, just to be the, "star reporter" is so sporting.

Christmas is celebrated as the birth of Christ ... an all-knowing
   God is everywhere at all times ... don't think of that –;
Because He has a Recording Angel recording all he finds ... he
   records when my recorder is turned to off and all down pat!!!
When thinking to make sport, we gather to play all the recordings
   back ... so many voices, a jumbled mess ...
Really beginning to think our judgment not so very sound ...
   knowing God's recording will be PLAIN, TRUE, CLEAR,
      the very best.

The reason tape recorders are such a wanted gift it seems, of
    most interest to one person is another person's life ...
With a tape recorder ... if not part of the conversation ... don't get
    miffed ... just flip the switch ... stir up more strife –;
God's Recording Angel doesn't get in on just a part ... he never
    misses an evil deed or bad word spoken;
He records our life ... our words and deeds from finish to start ...
    Oh, MY !!! – I never thought or realized ... forget the little, tiny
    invisible tape recorder ... It's as if I've just awoken!!!
        For Christmas ... You choose, of your love just a token:
        The Recording Angel won't have to ... turn
                                Another
                                PAGE!!!
Matthew 12:36-37

Happy New Year

Happy New Year ... happy New Year
And a year that's prosperous;
Greetings you hear far and near;
Returning them, you just must.

What about when the new wears off;
Will we still greet the same?
At disappointments ... will we scoff;
In trust, exalt Jesus' name?

Happiness isn't always the same;
To each, there's a difference ...
Happiness to one is a game,
To others, a defense.

Happy New Year ... hearts without fear;
Face what else lies ahead ...
Knowing their lives the Lord will steer;
Faith lives with all else dead.

An Irish Valentine

My Irish heritage … for this I'm ever –
    thankful –;
There's depth of heart – home and love are
    so much a part;
If matters not if you're Irish … there's nothing –
    work or play … that's dull …
That spark that's always an integral part … of
    heart – is the start.

Valentine's Day … with the Irish is an everyday
    affair …
Through hardships monumental … famine and drought –
    having to leave the Emerald Isle –;
Still, what was deep set in brave loving hearts …
    coming to a new country – to dare;
A little bit of Ireland was brought with each one –
    in laughter and smiling eyes from there.

Appreciation of family and friends – love of God –
    runs strong – defeating despair –;
Being able to make even work fun … is an ability
    not many inherit;
A song in the heart – knowing difficulties are
    surmountable – with faith in God, is not so rare …
Mostly you think one of Irish lineage – even though missing
    the language lilt – A Valentine without a care.

For: My Four Valentines

To My Valentines

Happy Valentine's Day to all ...
I say ... "I do love you" –
Each name, I don't have time to call;
As kitchen ... I pursue.

"Proof of the pudding's in the eating"!
They say it ... so do I ...
We all, our culinary arts did try –
Hard work ... and soon goodbye.

"Presents" are usually...edibles;
For this is what we like ...
We'll eat... enjoy ourselves and sigh;
When finished ... need, to hike.

Wish our boys were here ... as of old;
To enjoy all we've fixed ...
Memories of all we bake are ... told;
When here ... they have their pick.

Be my Valentine ... all the time;
Loving ... each so dearly ...
In a hurry ... it's hard to rhyme;
Suppertime ... here ... nearly.

When the Present is the Past

Springtime … yard work just begins …;
Flowers to plant as the sun rays descend;
Dew on the grass dries so very fast –;
Hot weather is coming … winter is past;
Severely cold days will be remembered …;
Perhaps, as only chilly weather in December.

It's always been so with man –;
Forever thinking back … as far as he can;
Neglecting to appreciate the present state …
Much of the time until … it's too late.
When the present has become a part of … the past;
Glossed over by time, it becomes, "The Good Old Days"
    … perfect at last!!!

A Good Day!

Mother's Day was a good day ... it was today –;
Though well pump certainly acted up ...
Water flooding over well-house floor ... to lay;
And a lot of finishing touches to dinner before we sup.

We dressed for church ... were ready to go ...;
Plans changed quickly ... with pump gone awry –;
Into our stay-at-home clothes ... with hand tools in tow.
Parts places closed ... with no place to buy.

We had good Mother's Day dinner ...;
Since much was prepared in advance –;
A very good thing ... having so much to hinder;
Never one to leave a big dinner's plans to chance.

A Mother's Day filled with love ...;
Our two daughters were home with us –;
Both sons living in other states ... were unable to come;
But, called by phone ... visiting – not in a rush.

It isn't the gifts which are inevitably given;
But, the love which prompts love to a mother –;
The effort put forth ... adds much to living ...;
The Bible way ... is in honor, preferring one another.

Preparation

When it's vacation time ... and planning to go on a journey;
There are preparations to be made ...;
Excitement is experienced ... with yearnings –;
Making ready for the trip ... not to be delayed.

Vacations, with all that's required ... familiar to all;
Looking forward to a change ... won't be denied –;
Yet, glad to be home again – all can recall ...;
Where to go – what to do ... one must decide.

There's one trip we all must take ...;
Either by death or at ... the Lord's return –;
Heaven or Hell is a choice we all must make;
It's a personal choice ... in God's word we learn.

In God's Holy Word, we're given signs of the time;
To herald the good news ... Christ's second coming is near.
Read your Bible – study ... then in the news you'll find –;
Many prophecies already fulfilled ... to hearts held dear.

To live with Christ in Heaven for aye ...;
Comes by accepting Christ as Saviour ... the only door.
By grace through faith – with repentance is the Biblical way.
Salvation is a gift, not by works – just accept it ... nothing more.

A "vacation" forever in Heaven will be ...;
To all who make the right choice and preparation ;
Christ died shedding His blood on Calvary for you and me –;
Those choosing Christ ... an eternal home in Heaven, their
    destination.

To delay in making preparation ... lies great danger ...;
God sent Christ to die in our stead ... the greatest, "Love Story".

Labor Holiday
or
Holiday Labor?

Labor Day is looked forward to as a holiday –
  before settling down as the year before does lay –
All students are anxious, for the long
  weekend – before the anticipation of Thanksgiving –.
But, of all the "holidays," it seems it is
  just as it's called, "Labor Day" –;
So much to get done – in a run – so short a
  time –
A long weekend – crammed with living.

Why so many things left, until, "Labor Day" …
  can you say …
Perhaps, the name itself gets in the way – of
  carefree holiday … should be "rest while you may."
Many things are put on the shelf until, "Labor
  Day" … unless rain gets in the way …
Tuesday morning – back to work – what a
  "quirk" – worked the long weekend – without pay!

Hot Weather

Would you please turn on the fan ... it's so very hot!
The fan's already on ... believe it or not ...;
Storm clouds are heavy and dark −;
Yet, the chance for rain seems stark.
Everything's dry − scorched − burning up;
Oh, for a shower of rain ... to fill earth's cup.

Dust blowing ... sifting − powdering sand;
Grime on everything ... nothing is banned.
With perspiration and exhaustion ... air seems rare;
Humidity so heavy ... breathing's a dare.
Dispositions changing ... caustic to sour ...;
The effect of heat on man's life has great power.

Time for air-conditioning − or suffer the heat;
It seems while in the sun ... the heat is sweet ...;
But, inside the office or home ... or even in the shade;
Not enjoying the heat ... to the sun is seldom laid −;
Fans and air-conditioners continue to run;
So many disdain the heat ... while loving the sun!

Nature

Summer is a Fun Time

Don't you think summer is a fun time?
Usually vacations are taken then ...;
Everything is so changed from the usual grind –;
Schedules are rearranged ... and easy to bend.

Straw hats and bare feet ... as the sun does beat;
With ice cream and lemonade – the heat just fades;
Looking for a place under the big oak tree, finding a seat;
All passing by, remark ..."My! You have it made!"

They weren't looking on while work was going on ...;
Yard and garden work are exhausting – work never done.
What may appear a restful scene ... is energy just gone;
But, anyway you look at it, summertime is fun!

But, the Calendar and Almanac??

Hard to plan an early garden … with the weather
   changing so …
You can never tell if there'll be … rain, hail, sleet
   or snow –;
Seems it's time … looking at calendar and almanac – the
   usual things by which we go;
Waiting for weather report … hopefully – sunshine and
   rain … anything other – a gardener's foe.

The date on calendar and almanac so stated … time
   to plant – with garden tools so aided;
Plants are in … tomatoes, peppers, cabbage … that's
   just to begin …
Seeds put in rows later … careful to plant where last
   year – something different had been –;
Each year … with gardening it's never the same…
   only the anticipation and expectation abide.

Much ado … when the news' reports say … "Hail is on the
   its way" –;
Hurrying and scrambling … for jars – the lot without
   delay … plants must be covered night or day;
Sometimes, it seems best to just forget … making a
   garden and do what many do … or say …
Yet, each year … when springtime is near … enthusiastically
   heading for the garden with renewed zest!!!

In gardening for sure … one is made to know and
   plainly see –;
It's the Lord, our God who controls the elements …
   that be …
The more … "acu" the weather report becomes … it has
   always seemed to me;
The farther off the prediction … for God just let us
   see – control and change of weather are up to Him not us.

A Blessing From God

The sun is so hot … the ground so dry – the dust flying
    upward … toward the sky;
Dust blowing with the hot south wind … no moisture in
    the air – not a cloud in sight …
There's such a haze … you can't keep from wiping your
    eyes … unable to see the birds as they fly by;
Heat waves rising up from the parched earth … as from
    an oven … the sun exerts its right …

Plants in garden, flowers and shrubs … even the trees
    are wilted and dry …;
All things growing are droopy and withered … where
    roots are shallow;
It's almost as if the whole of creation gives off a
    tumultuous sigh –;
Each sound … resounding back as a tightly stretched
    drum … the ground being fallow.

When the needed rain comes … such thankfulness and
    rejoicing it brings …
Refreshing and cooling … slowly turning everything
    parched back to green –
Man has accomplished much that is noteworthy …
    not failing his own praises to sing.
But, to God we can pray … only He sends the rain …
    no matter the vastness of the scientific scheme.

Quiet

It's quiet ... while it really isn't ...;
Hearing sounds – but, in the distance –;
Spirit and heart are soothed in the sun;
While wind ripples the water with resistance.

Shadows play upon trees in light ...;
Butterflies hovering where flowers are in bloom –;
Wind blowing leaves at times out of sight;
Warm sun's ray will turn hot soon.

Noise in the air suspended ... not coming near;
The quiet soothes the spirit ... closer to God;
For a time drawn away ... from many things to hear –;
No concern to me ... as head begins to nod.

Oh! to live with spirit and body at one ...;
Living close to God through Christ, His Son –;
Is the nearest to Heaven ... on earth to be done;
Until we're in Heaven ...when earth's race is run.

Quiet ... yet, if you listen ... not really quiet;
Listening with your ears... not heart, to what surrounds;
Birds, chickens, dogs and bees ... noise a riot;...
Though thoughts can override all outward sounds.

Quiet ... it won't be in our Heavenly home ...;
So much rejoicing and praises in song –;
It will all be peace and joy ... no more we'll roam;
Nothing good we've done ... all through Christ for which
    we long.

Early Morning

Early morning ... early morning before the
    sun comes up ...
Not meaning by this – six or seven o'clock, but ...
    four or five ...
First thing to do ... plug in the coffee pot
    and then out on the patio with a cup.
So refreshing ... to take a few sips to wake
    you up – thanking the Lord for being alive.

Listening to the quiet is ... quite a soothing
    experience –;
Now and then, some sound not noticed
    in the course of the day ...
With rushing and turmoil – the usual
    way of life – quiet of morning has no adherence –
Like a rooster crowing in the distance –
    sounding out of place and far away ...

Frogs in your own private lake ... mostly
    quiet – but, now and then, a "hmm-belly-deep" – very
        stout –
The cool soft air and morning breeze help to
    make for satisfaction – that nobody sees ...
A prayer uttered so quietly – but knowing the
    Lord does hear ... there's no doubt –;
Thankful and asking His protection and help as
    the quiet dissipates with the early morning breeze.

In Time

The rain came … just in time …
To sprout the seeds – every kind.

Fall gardens are much more fun –;
Not so many weeds – the garden overrun.

If frost comes early or very late …
With garden of greens – doesn't matter the date.

God gives the sunshine and the rain;
Our gardens grow – as God's blessings flow.

No matter if experienced gardener or not –;
The weather has no favorites – mattering not a jot.

If God doesn't bless the work that is done;
Just a lot of wasted time, in the heat of the sun.

Gardening time, we get everything ready …;
Such excitement … even the air is heady.

We watch to see when the little seeds sprout ;
After awhile – we gather tools and are digging about.

Vegetables all kinds – from a garden, our own;
Seems so much better … than ordered by phone.

Everyone should have of earth a little plot,
To grow vegetables – an enjoyment that's man's lot.

Salad Greens

There are numerous kinds of salads –;
When compared to wild greens ... they're found pallid;
Polk Salad to many ... the very best ...;
Either plain or eggs scrambled in a gourmet fest.

Much of the enjoyment of the wild greens is the foraging;
Fun in the searching ... preparation, then gorging ...;
The fresh air and walking to find the wild tender greens –
Whets the appetite ... making all taste better it seems.

One must take care in trampling through the woods;
A snake might be basking where you wouldn't think he would.
If you have dog which likes to go along ...;
He is a great help – keeping things from going wrong.

Sometimes there are mosquitoes, chiggers and even ticks;
You learn self-preservation by a few tricks ...;
A can of insect repellent ... saves itching many a day –;
Then off to the woods ... is only just play.

A Great God has provided abundantly ... if we would only look;
Some writers have a qualified a list of wild foods in their book.
Around the world, God has placed wild plants and herbs for food;
If one will only search and look – with an adventurous mood.

Berry Picking

…Blackberries …
Vines on the ground to lie;
Stickers and chiggers –;
…Blackberry pie!!

…Blackberries …
Find a good patch –,
Stickers and chiggers;
…Blackberry pie!!

Just won't pick again,
Too miserable a time;
Chigger Tox – Cortizone Five,
… Blackberry pie!!

Next year won't be as bad,
Stickers and chiggers –;
Oh, well! Berries to be had!
… Blackberry pie!!

Grandmother's Garden

What's different about Grandmother's garden?
There's rhubarb, shallots ... old-fashioned herbs ...
Of course, there's turnips, plus other greens –;
Not complete without garlic and string beans.

Grandmother always knows the very best recipes ...
She has her own way of cooking ... could baffle a scientist.
Some unique way ... she cooks without measuring ...
So, in the strictest sense of the word – it's "very secret."

Grandmother always has time for loved ones and friends;
Always time for Bible study and much prayer.
Though she'd frail in body, yet of her own vulnerability
    she's very aware.
Up in years ... but, strong of faith in the Lord.

Lily Pads

Wind blowing softly – lily pads, floating on the
    lake … pink and shades of green –;
Makes a cool place and shade for the fish
    to hide – seems at times – must there reside!
Tiny little ripples … blowing the direction
    of the wind … causing a sheen –;
If only things could always be …as peaceful
    as the lakeside – there just to abide.

It matters not if the fish are in school
    or have been;
Just a nibble now and then … enough
    to keep the interest – as to when?
Always thinking … after this cast –
    I'll cast – once again –;
Nothing to hurry or bother – just lazily
    fish until you've filled your cup …

If the stringer is full … at the end of
    the day …
So much the better – fish to cook; but,
    nevertheless, such a glorious day – filled with rest;
Mind and body relaxed so much – for
    tranquility like this – one doesn't have to pay …;
Such quiet – birdsong in the distance – blowing
    on the breeze – filling life with renewed zest.

Apple Blossoms

Apple blossoms blooming –
Fragrant – the essence
Not out of a bottle …
Blowing in the breeze –
Bees are buzzing everywhere,
The pollen making us sneeze!

Too Anxious

So anxious to get at gardening …;
As soon as the weather turns warm –;
After the winter spent in sewing and darning;
Just to get outside in the sunshine where the bees swarm.

Too soon the … nights turn cold again …;
Plants are in the ground … though not upward bound;
At night, covering plants with anything at hand;
It's never good to plant too early … in the cold ground.

Tiny seeds need sunshine and rain …;
Sprouting, then to peep through … they can be found;
With cold days and nights … a garden never gains –;
Should wait until warm weather … advise is sound.

Poetic Forms

Wisdom
(Sonnet)

Alone – alone ... forlorn ... how can that be?
Converging – thronging millions everywhere;
Not daring ... lonely ... and too blind to see;
Removed from all that surrounds ... not to care;
Feeling never free ... living locked inside ...
Sand castle dreams ... emotions exhausted.
Such unreal dreaming ... drifting ... with no guide;
Surrounded yet, ... companionship ... foisted;
Many memories ... though they do elude;
Time heals ... physician ... not the enemy ...
Anxiety destroys ... forever shrewd ...
The Lord accepts our faith ...the remedy;
Though tossed in tumult with another's rage;
Seeks to survive ... with wisdom of the sage.

The Testing Teacher
(Sonnet)

The testing teacher though weary and worn ;
Has everything ready ... waiting forlorn ...!
In drifts one, two – then coming in, a few!
Have to get started – don't have all day –;
For those who are late ... we can't delay –.
Teacher must start – so much time for each part.
Bookwork's to be done – no day for a lark!
So many absent – sick to my heart!
There will have to be make-up test –;
That means, next week – no time for rest.
Must – to continue, at the same pace;
Almost, running over myself, in the race.
Too much work for one person to do;
You'd think the test was to benefit you!

The Pepper
(Sonnet)

The pepper for cooking an excellent choice;
Flavors many foods – salads and such –
Some like red, yellow or green …
They are mild, hot or sweet …
Cooked or fresh, they're much in demand;
Many different varieties are in different lands.
A pepper will certainly spice things up;
At home or abroad – wherever you sup …
It changes the flavor adding its part;
Such fun to cook with, from the finish to the start.
Not only the flavor is enhanced so much;
But, all the color added – using one or the bunch.
Of all the vegetables to come to the kitchen
A good part of its job is a "flavorful" mission.

Without Price
(Sonnet)

True love proves true – whatever else to rue;
Mattering not the demands, to withstand –;
True love will not be foolishly pursued;
Always it seeks ... not knowing where to find,
As elusive moonbeams, yet strong as death.
Love's bonds continue – wrapping hearts the more;
For time goes past this way once – keeping score;
All remedies, to change – what's been – folklore.
True love bears and over all obstacles – soars.
Love to be true ... is only up to you ...
Regardless if alone ... some gone before;
True love exalted ... has purity due ...
Without price – yet, labor freely given;
No recompense is sought – none to be bought!

Someone Other
(Sonnet)

Lamenting … still the fact you must be you;
All such varied aspects … of twists and turns;
Maneuvering to be someone pursued …
Going through life, elusive dreams … yearn;
Only to be someone other … not – me –.
No faults made aware – nor none to despair
Another to be … perfection to see …
When being someone other – faults still there.
Manifested shortcomings … magnified …
Never diminished by closing of eyes;
To self, always be true – you are unique;
Hypocrisy will collapse self-respect …
Look at yourself … another look to take;
All God's handiwork … He didn't forsake.

On Depression
(Sonnet)

Body bent, head bowed, eyes cast down:
Seeing not what surrounds, of earth's beauty;
Looking through windows where all remains dim;
Depression carried as if it's a duty ...
Nothing of color registers ... to pierce the fog;
Kind words and deeds never reach where they need,
Day and night the same ... sinking in the bog.
Heart's asleep to what is now ... body freed;
An inventory of all that's been ... summed up ...
Cannot suffice for what ... does lie ahead;
While the past, so much of life has disrupt,
Faith in the Lord, forgiveness alleviates dread.
    Christ died on the Cross that we might have life;
    Believing ... we might have it more abundantly.

Hurry! Hurry!
(Pantoum)

Because I tried to care for my children,
To keep up, I was always so worn out ...
Yet, never, getting done what was needed,
Sometimes, in circles, I was turned about.

To keep up, I was always so worn out ...
Never getting done all that was needed;
Sometimes in circles I was turned about;
Like riding a merry-go-round ... around.

Never getting done all that was needed;
In a hurry from morn until the night,
Like riding a merry-go-round around
With no place to stop; therefore, no exit!

In a hurry from morn until the night,
Then to rest until the day breaks anew!
With no place to stop; therefore, no exit!
Sleep clinging to eyelids, tired through and through.

Then to rest until the day breaks anew!
Up to start the day with the clock's alarm,
Sleep clinging to eyelids, tired through and through;
They need breakfast before leaving for school.

Up to start the day with the clock's alarm!
Wish I'd gotten one with the snooze devise;
They need breakfast before leaving for school.
Sleepy, I should get up before lunch!

Wish I'd gotten one with the snooze devise;
Never seem to get done what was needed,
Sleepy, I should get up before lunch!
Because I tried to care for my children.

Monsoon of the Spirit
(Villanelle)

Through Christ ... God does for the spirit of man,
When He is accepted as one's Saviour,
What the monsoon does for a thirsty land:

Refreshing ... bringing to life as it were ...
That which seemed worthless ... of no use and dead;
Dearth of heart's spirits until the new birth:

All things are passed away ... when Spirit led;
Water of the monsoon makes flowers bloom,
Grass grows so tall in a dry desert bed;

A herd of elephants could hide where foliage looms;
An abundant life in Christ knows no bounds:
Looking up in faith: morning, night and noon.

Monsoon fills desert with many new sounds;
All life teeming with gladness ... rejoicing
Thankful for life-giving water's full bounds.

The Spirit made alive in Christ takes wing ...
Rejoicing in abundant life, He died to give:
On Calvary's Tree, He took away sin's sting.
Redemption's story is what we're to sing.
Helping flowers bloom that will never die.

The Storm's Eye
(Villanelle)

The storms in spring seem worse than storms in fall;
Strong winds and fierce wildfires, flooding and hail;
One never knows when or on whom they call.

Flames, waves and winds enormously tall,
At times, breaking what's been measurement's scale;
The storms in spring seem worse than storms in fall.

No recourse, but prayer, in corridor's hall,
Turning to the Lord for help in storm's gale;
One never knows when or on whom they call.

Without faith in God, hearts shrink to appall;
With calm in the "eye of the storm" – fear does pale;
The storms in spring seem worse than storms in fall.

Faith with prayer can penetrate doubt's wall,
Seeking safety, not weak … female or male;
One never knows when or on whom they call.

Love and trust bring rest in storm's bitter gale;
While, without it, human spirit's wail;
The storms in spring seem worse than storms in fall,
One never knows when or on whom they call.

Decisions ... Decisions
(Satire)

Being in the position I am ... so many decisions to make ...;
With even ... the country's security at stake –;
A big decision to face ... each day I awake;
What color hair for today ... as this color I forsake.

Changing color won't be fun – on the campaign trail having to run
But, I'll need a lot of colors ... leave out none ...;
With so many people and cameras, may have to add another color
    when done –;
Hair color is so important ... on train or bus ... in or out of the sun

Best to match hair color to where we go ...;
Speaking to a group older citizens ... color to seek ... grey – just
    so;
When speaking to the younger crowd –;
More blond or brown than grey ... color subdued ... not loud.

Hmmm ... what will the color be today ...brown, dun or just grey!
Hey, Al, where's this speech you say ...?
Oh, Oooooh ... we're speak to the "blind" today ...
You mean the ones who, "can't see" ... I can leave it its own way.

I tell you what ... no hair color today I'll wear ...;
To not have to be so burdened with big decisions is rare;
It isn't fair ... "I've been called the, "great Pretender" –;
But, really ... I really don't know the color of my own hair!!!"

Truth
(Skeltonic Verse)

Truth is of the essence,
It speaks for itself,
Looking right nor left;
Straight without a welt,
It is never by stealth;
Poverty or wealth ...
To character it's melt,
Whatever is dealt,
To none has it knelt;
By many it's felt,
In some lives it dwells;
By too few it's held;
Others never met,
On them doesn't set,
So, what use to fret?
Answers you won't get!
Never feel their debt!
Leaving on a jet!!!
When they're caught in net;
But, never regret,
With thinking all wet;
Truth, never a pet;
Its substance won't let!
Stands ever true, yet.
Regardless what's said,
No matter the dread;
Never will be dead;
Deceit hasn't wed;
On it never fed,
Can't be wayward led!
Brings to light instead;
Answers every head;
Evil caught in web!
The wicked it shreds,
Their ego it treads;
It will leave no vent,
For on light it's bent,
Cannot circumvent ...
Character can dent –

A scoundrel – not gent!
Proof ... not just a hint;
When influence was lent;
Deceit definitely meant,
Stiff-necked, won't repent,
High reaches the stench,
Though deep the trench,
It never will wince;
Removed fog that's dense,
Sin's curtain it rends,
Example it sends ...
With patience bends;
Own, "sifter" and, "scout";
Other things wear out,
Turned and turned about;
Truth never brings doubt;
Always remains stout!
Even though there's gout;
Never hides to pout ...
Though exposures mount!
No detour of route,
Truth you cannot taunt;
Matters not the bout;
Nothing has more clout!
Christ, of Truth, the Fount;
Men of no account ...
Totally depraved is he,
Born in sin ALL be;
Isn't hard to see;
Christ will set man free,
Repentance is the need;
It's by faith ... not deed!
All, born of Adam's seed;
On Calvary, Christ died;
Believers not denied;
Christ's blood ... sin does hide;
ALL in TRUTH – not pride.

A Ghazal

Sitting here in the study; I see many things.
The piano is here ... so sometimes, in here we sing.

The radio broadcast is recorded here, so it is a
     preaching room, too.
There are shelves of books ... many, never read,
     though not new.

A double desk is built across one whole wall.
There's a chair pulled up to each divided stall.

Across the room, there's a typewriter and desk.
Just a little space, but, to me, a writer's fest.

There's a typewriter on the big desk, been there
     for years.
Typing up notes for sermons, one frequently hears.

This room certainly is of multi-purpose use.
With all the clutter ... could call it abuse.

There's family pictures, book-ends of onyx,
     cowboy statues scattered around.
A good sorting and spring cleaning ...when time
     is found.

Somebody ... would think everything there should
  be kept.
Discarding such treasures ... you must watch your
  step.
So many activities here have taken place.
Family singing hymns ... while one plays with grace.

Many memories are stored within these four walls.
Much more stored in boxes ...what ... one can't recall.

Maxine, much of what's here needs to be thrown out!
Thoughts of good times would have more room to turn
  about.

An Alphabetical Discussion

A   young man, thinking of enlisting, worked on An Army base.

B   Said, 'My Boy! Best you just work, then leave the place!'

C   Said, 'Can't see why you'd join when you like your work.'

D   Said, 'Don't you hate to miss out on all the benefits and perks!'

E   Said, 'Everywhere you look some are standing at attention.'

F   Said, 'From what I hear … there's a pension.'

G   Said, 'That's Good, go for it, for an army we do need!'

H   Said, 'Do they Have and will they Have … plenty there to lead?'

I   Said, 'Imagine just what chaos without anyone in charge!'

J   Said, 'Just what it would be if each gave the other a discharge.'

K   Said, 'Khaki or whatever color won't please all!'

L   Said, 'In Lieu … so many colors to appall!'

M   Said, 'Many Might want to take a vote …'

N   Said, "With No one in authority … None to take Note!'

O   Said, 'Our Uncle Sam is getting Old!"

P   Said, 'Perhaps, he is getting old, but, he's still rated bold.'

Q   Said, 'Keep Quiet … perhaps, it's the best.'

R   Said, 'Really, you think so?'

S   Said, 'Sit Still, Stay awhile and watch how things go.'

T   Said, 'Training, Tracking, marching, goes on just so.'

U   Said, 'Unaware are the new recruits, Unsuspecting of what's in store.'

V   Said, 'Remember Varied … Very strict discipline's such
    a chore.'

W   Said, 'Wear the uniform proudly … no matter how many
    places in the world you're scattered and sent!'

X   Said, 'At X-rated … anything, don't ever … even hint!'

Y   Said, "You, Your morals tell on You … what demeanor
    You present!'

Z   Said, 'Remember Zorro? He should be an example! Don't
    Look to the President! Zorro was identified by the
    mark of his signature … a, "Z".

Thought-Provoking

"Love Not Money"

Love of money, never a stumble,
Aggressively finding its path.
Quietly …winding without a rumble,
Shadowing, pressed closely, without wrath.

Deceiving, … not to be found out,
Yet, is manifest in the game
Interest with covetousness on route
Envy it is, whatever name.

Love of money is the root of evil,
All evil, though different – the same
Without heart, denial feeble
Envy evil with sin, inflame.

Matters not the path that's chosen
For basic facts we need not train,
Human nature in time frozen
Never living is to … refrain.

Faith in Christ, a new mind and heart,
With values ordered, changed about.
The root of evil is … love of money …
Not MONEY.

Greed

Always creeping closer is greed:
Hid by shadows ... but, still lurking;
Escape wisdom's path proceed ...
Tarrying from wisdom it will lead.

Wisdom heeded ... greed's greatest foe:
As it wields its engulfing cloak;
First glance, if missed, one may not know;
Until its fires, with envy stoke.

Discerning spirit, watchful eyes:
See what escaped ... though only small,
Pushed aside, all wisdom defied!
Rebellion's path feels bitter gall.

Wisdom outweighs all stage performance:
For peace ... greed never has the price;
A Christ-filled heart, life will enhance.
Greed ... a much used devil's devise.

As a man thinketh so is he:
A man is what he is inside,
Abundance of man's heart Christ does see;
All sin and greed, Christ's blood does hide.

Depression's the devil's Pit

Depression is the devil's pit …
Discouraging us to look up;
To God Who on His Throne does sit,
Desiring us with Him to sup.

The world holds so much of beauty,
That God gave for man to enjoy;
Hills, mountains, lakes and the sea,
Flowers, birds, desert, so much there be;

Depression functions as an umbrella
Keeping a dark shadow between you and the sun,
Only faith pervades the pit the devil dug,
Truth's in the "Light of the World," God's only Son.

To please God, we walk by faith and not by sight.
Not looking to self or the arms of the flesh,
Depression is not looking up, but, only to see the pit the
    devil dug;.
So, let faith lift from the pit into light.

Without faith, it's impossible to please God,
Faith is the opposite of despair …
Depression is not from God … man of the sod,
Depression is used by the devil to snare.

Guilt

How does guilt cause one to feel?
The Bible says the guilty flee when no man pursueth;
Guilt is strongly felt … when knowing right is real;
Guilt is never comfort … whatever one doeth.

Blaming others always is guilt's characteristic.
To justify self … even to senses bereft –;
Criticize all to appall – but dastardly
Guilt causes one to lie … all reasoning left.

If one could see themselves when clothed in guilt
That no covers enough or … thick,
To reach into a guilt-ridden heart.
And give peace of mind … slowly or quickly.

Guilt causes blame to shift so easily
To ones who before were counted blameless.
Guilt dries up a person to measly –
All who observe … know guilt, though nameless.

The Lord will forgive when His conditions are met.
A person must repent … that's why Christ was sent;
God cannot despise a repentant heart – His standards set.
His plan … one to be right must turn and repent.

Busybody

Much we've heard about the busybody.
Tending to all the business not her own.
Amazing how she has so much time free
Everyone knows she has much to do at home.

Goes from door to door where she's been before,
Perhaps, there'll be something more of gossip!
Anxious to see if they have more in store,
She should know that all think, she should button her lip.

While a busybody does drift around
Other bodies are busy … so much work,
Working at the jobs so easily found
To be a busybody, work one must shirk.

Spread the gossip, spread it thick – all may not stick
Like planting seed some for the birds, some to grow.
A busybody likes learning new tricks
Always broadcasting, words as seeds to sow.

Some seeds sown – the wind does carry away,
Spread, never to be gathered again.
Like the busybody's game she does play
Spreading busybody "germs," as the sand.

Paranoid

Paranoia ... can become as a hidden enemy – a
   terrible tragedy –;
Causing suspicion ... where there should be –
   none ...
Keeping life at a miserable stand – unsure as
   you began;
It will undermine one's own security ...
   and integrity.

Each answers to the Lord – don't expect from
   people a reward.
Stand firmly on the teachings of God's Holy
   Word;
Listening to Him ... the other won't be –
   heard ...
With heart in tune to God ... all unfounded fear,
   disregard.

When you feel such paranoia you want to run
   and hide;
Remember God is over all ... just rest as you
   recall ...
There's no place His love can't reach – nothing ...
   it can't forestall.
Knowing the devil is subject to God ... you're on
   the winning side.

Don't be so taken back ... to where very doubt
   doth stem;
There are real fears to all – as through life goes
   one and all.
Faith in God sees us through ... though we stumble
   and we fall ...
Trusting ... resting in the arms of God – paranoia
   will grow dim.

...Others have their fears ... the same as –
   you ...
Try being a help ... feeling secure yourself – tell
   them of Christ –;
Perhaps, no one before ... ever told them of Christ's
   great price;
Paranoia ... forgotten ... as Christ's work you
   pursue.

Getting What's Given

The attitude a person has toward life ... will
   determine the amount of pleasure enjoyed –;
Another way of saying the same ... you get
   out of anything what you put into it;
If all the important issues are ignored ...
   instead of pleasure, there looms a great void ...
Attitude toward life – responsibility and
   obligation determine ... the pleasure you get.

Attitude accounts for much ... God's word
   teaches such ... yet, still we resist –;
Grumbling and complaining about all
   we're called upon to do;
Becoming discouraged ... hindering all
   progress ... causing others to desist ...
Our attitude – concerning self and others – is
   of the essence ... a life of faith – best to pursue.

Really?

So … you say you're sorry …
For hurt caused by caustic words sown ;
You say it – and say it's so –;
Why not act as though …?
As words with actions go –;
Just doesn't seem to converge …
Really … when sorrow is true –
And really it's so … one can surely know.

Self-Competition

Did you ever think ... why in ALL things a
    person must compete with someone else –;
Only some things are aptly attuned – to see
    if you or someone else will be the winning one.
With most things in life – competing with
    self will be the most rewarding – and best;
When we work to improve on our own performance
    ... then we've matured some.

Competition ... if not with a spirit approved
    by God – honesty, honor and rules respected –;
A sense of camaraderie should pervade any event –
    whatever our talent – of God it was lent ...;
Or it does nothing to impart good character –
    which God does of His children expect.
Courage to give of your best ... in whatsoever
    you do – you may surpass others – but it could be you!

Competition can be great ... if a person his
    egotism – when winning – can regulate –;
If always referring to ourselves – and our abilities –
    others are hesitant to commend us even if they could!
The Bible teaches – let another praise us – not
    we ourselves ... it could fester hate.
God is the One to judge ... we need do the
    best we can ... trying as we should.

Should I??

Should I be interested in what others …
  do?
Should I take part in what has to do with
  you –?
Certainly each one has a private life …
  lives partly to himself …
But, a goodly portion … to share – with
  others is left.

Best to be alert … so much dreaming
  desert – know what's going on – lest you be hurt;
After all – the only way to get things done …
  is by being alert;
How can one know … action to take or
  decisions to make …
If from the real world our mind does
  forsake – with mind in space – sanity's stake.

Courage with faith in God ... solves many
    a dilemma ...
Trusting Him to care and LEAD ... most
    surely fulfills our every need;
All should have sound thoughts – based
    on God's Word – always ready to learn and discern –;
Not ignoring what's going on around ... and
    whatever found – never from reality to turn.

No one lives entirely to himself ... all
    lives touch others – no one bereft;
When hearing humanity's cry for help ...
    never should it fall on ears selectively deaf –;
We must face life ... as it really is ...
    not pretending what isn't ... IS ...
Secure and always safe in our Saviour's
    care ... facing up to life – all other business is
      His!

Feeling Sorry For Myself

Nothing to live for ... is that a fact...?
If you had some dread disease you'd take that back;
As long as God gives life and breath ...
There's some reason ... why one escapes death!
Find something to do ... look all around –;
Others in worse shape than you ... many Hell-bound.
Get busy serving the Lord ... through people ...;
Much of the Lord's work is outside a church steeple.
Living one's life dedicated to serving the Lord ...
Even though it's promised ... yet, not serving for a reward;
Not one misdeed or one that's good, escapes the All-Seeing Eye;
We answer to Him here ... and after we die –;
A life of faith is abundant with love ...;
Though tired and worn ... strength is given from God above.

Who's ... To Blame?

There must be, there hast to be ... someone to blame
    for what's happened to me ...;
Choosing someone ... to blame ... there's many the same ...
    cheering my own voice –;
It matters not if what I choose is what I see ... or
    seems to be;
Don't confuse with all the facts ... my imagination –
    nothing lack – hearing what is best, the choice.

When it's pouring down rain ... to go out, means getting
    drenched ...
Ice and snow ... makes a body shiver, shake as it grows
    cold;
With no rain and sun shining hot in summer ... makes
    for drought and stench –;
Strong winds destroy life ... trees and vegetations ...
    sturdy buildings do fold.

A little foresight and protection can guard a person
    from the rain, sun or snow –;
But, situations in life where WE must decide – can't
    be the fault of others ... even though nigh;
Sin and troubles have been with us from the beginning,
    we know;
But, trusting the Lord to take care and lead ... is always
    where peace doth lie.

Keeping oneself close to the Lord ... willing to do His
    bidding;
No matter the circumstances ... right isn't accomplished
    where fervor is slight ...;
Faith with obedience is pleasing to God ... wavering
    vanquished ... doubts ridding –;
Trusting our Saviour ... steps not to falter ... though led
    through the darkest of nights.

Remembering

At times, forgetfulness can be a blessing
   indeed.
Things in the past ... which hurt you
   so –;
But, forgotten if you pay too little
   heed –
Memory, when upsetting, can be a –
   detrimental foe.

Forgiveness can come ... but, still may
   never forget ...
The difference ... between is ever so ...
   much –
God help us to forgive ... from a heart
   filled with love ...
But, to always forget everything and all –
   our mind would be gone – we'd need
     be locked away – out of reality's touch.

My World

My own world, a world just for me ... there's no one of
    importance but "me, myself and I" ... anywhere I see;
I did this ... I do that ... I don't like this ... I don't
    like that ...;
I don't like him ... I don't like her ...
    I don't like them ... don't ask me why!
When I look all around ... there's nothing I see that's
    worthy of me – but, as servant or a mat!

My world is little – not much bigger than I ... is small
    indeed, for everything outside my way impedes ...;
I don't know where I'm going or what I'll do – but one
    thing's for certain, I'll be my own guru –;
In my world I'm the only one who fits ... it's all for
    me or smaller recedes ...;
Just to live in my own little world ... that I do ... no
    one really matters but you know WHO!!!

Don't You Think?

(Conversation Between Two Thinkers)

Well ... what do you think?
Hmmm ... oh ... uh ...I don't know ...
Don't you think it's on the brink?
Yes, you expressed my sentiments just so!

Don't you believe that's the way it is?
Oh! ... uh ... hmmm ... I just don't know –;
Didn't you think what was his?
Yes, I suppose it's as the story goes.

Don't you think the story's exaggerated?
Oh ... I don't know ... what thinkest you?
In my opinion, it was vastly overrated ...;
Well then ... we think the same ... we really do.

Do you think one needs to think?
Oh, yes, but it takes so much time –;
Always so busy with other things ... I find ...
For me, it's easier – not to think ... easier on the mind.

God expects us to study His word ... pray and think.
With wisdom ... not accept all we hear ... or see at first glance.
Everything isn't always as it appears – when to the truth it
　　doesn't link.
God is LOVE and TRUTH ... never leads contrary to His
　　Word – no chance!

Just Listen

Just recall ... things you were taught when
    you were small ...
Of how Jesus would always be there ... because
    He died for you;
And those who cared for you ... you knew would
    never let you fall;
They were always there to make things right ...
    even as you grew.

Just listen to your heart ... you taught your
    children the same ...
Taught them to accept Christ in early life ...
    warning them of Hell's pit;
In teaching little ones right – you made many
    lessons a game;
Train up a child in the way he should go ...
    when he is old he will not depart from it.

Now listen to your own heart ... as you would
    wish them to do ...
Remember now ... your teaching to them and the
    same things you were taught –
Take time to LISTEN as memories come flooding
    back to you;
Our labors for right are never in vain ... but
    with Christ's blood, He our salvation bought.

Sacrifices of God are a broken spirit; a broken
    and a contrite heart – God will not despise;
In repentance ... drawing closer to the Lord with
    faith, our spirit will be revived;
As we listen ... searching our own heart would be
    counted wise;
Checking to see ... perhaps, lessons we learned,
    have been cast aside.

Even in Changed Circumstances

Everything is different ... all is changed ...;
Life is still ever toward eternity moving –
Time has in life many things rearranged;
Yet, in turmoil and strife ... God's presence is soothing.

Whatever obstacles ... God's grace is sufficiently supplied;
Trust and faith reach to the great power in Heaven ...
God, who controls all things, can a broken heart and spirit revive;
Every good and perfect gift comes from God – without sin's leaven.

Changes in life many times leave a thread of fear ...
Unless there's abiding faith ... not seeing the ending is heartrending;
Where there's faith ... a God who knows ALL is forever near.
When placing our trust in Him ... one knows power from Heaven's
    descending.

Stopping to think and pray makes things easier understood ...
As to why such happenings have all come about –;
For those who love the Lord ... all things work for good;
Faith in the Lord, mattering not changes in route; ever trust, not
    doubt.

There Are Others!

Whenever self-pity ... comes forward – and
    asserts itself –;
Don't make room for its enlargement –
    festering more of the same.
Push it out of the way – placing it on the
    out-of-reach shelf ...;
For it never figures in life's real down –
    to-earth game.

Many others in circumstances much
    worse ...;
Could use some help ... if we only
    turn away from self –;
Stepping back – from self-pity ... another
    going first ...
Rejoicing in seeing the results of a
    helping hand – not being sustained –
      self-pity just left.

Do You Know?

Do you know there are some people – oh,
   so rough …?
 As long as they seem to have the …
   advantage –;
Only a coward … is tough on something
   helpless; … in his rage;
A pack of wolves will show their …
   stuff –;
Attacking a sick or small animal –
   that's their gauge …
There are people who are the same –
   but, call their bluff …
Pretty fast … they are ready to say – "It's enough!"

Nobody But Me!

There's just nobody … as important as I;
Nobody else really does count but me.
If that sounds terribly self-centered – so let it be;
For that attitude is so prevalent you see …

I must be first in EVERYTHING –
   or no self-esteem;
Don't you know self-esteem comes from the inside …?
Matters not what place we hold – or how we seem –
Self-esteem is for a fact – not based upon a vote –
   what others decide.

Always in thinking … first place always is self;
If gifts are in sight – naturally they should all be mine;
Matters not who's trodden upon and left …
Really must get a handle on this – to SEEM more refined.

Unless the heart be changed – priorities rearranged;
"SEEM," is the right word … to define …;
To be unselfish … a lot needs to change –;
The Lord first – others second – self – coming in behind.

Oh, it's hard to do … if you've only thoughts of you;
Asking God for His – always sufficient grace and help –;
Much progress … will be made – but only if you do …
It will take practice in doing – you may smart and whelp.

"Nobody but me," attitude – can be pushed aside;
With the desire to please God – in repentance of the heart,
Attributes – unselfish and helpful – will turn the tide,
Wasted years – so many gone – time to make a
   new start!

Political

The Road to There!

Politicians along with others who are called upon
    to lead ...;
If they're to gain the confidence of right thinking
    folk –;
Must prove themselves true in keeping their word or
    sow discord's seed;
Many are never ... but, some for awhile are deceived ...
    when learning of the duplicity, receive a jolt.

The old adage ... "If you don't know where you're going
    ... all roads lead there" ...;
Applies to one who ambles ... not knowing – unease with
    unrest, he's abundantly sowing –;
History always tells ... facts laid bare ... trust must
    be earned ... this occurs all too rarely;
There's much difference with dignity leading and showing
    where you're going, not just your weight throwing.

Most people are usually smarter than ... others seem
    to think ...;
Although many indolently drift ... carelessly are
    windswept ... whistling along –;
Yet, if stopping to think, their condoning of evil will
    have to be answered ... many break rank;
When face to face with God ... in light of His judgment –
    they'll wish they'd sung a different song.

Together

Together in the broader sense ...;
Though different ... much not the same –;
Yet, each individual ... with his own thoughts;
His freedom of expression ... with decisions fraught;
Coming together for the benefit of future generations –;
To set in motion the renewing of values and policies, many have
    shunned!

One party ... all for one ... one for all;
Values set forth ... under one umbrella it will fall;
Self-effacing ... in the promotion of values – consensus of the
    whole;
Many times, courage for right is evident ... speaking bold.
Biblical teaching, defining what's right come to light;
Dissension there'll always be ... when in the pursuit of right.

Opposing Ourselves

When we choose a path ... the opposite
   to what is right ...;
We oppose ourselves ... when we walk
   the road ... with obscuring light –;
Time may go on for short or long ...
   eventually catch up – some day or night.
Much happier life – to travel unhampered
   by unconfessed sins – basking in God's light!

Suppose a candidate when seeking
   office – when at the polls opposed himself ...;
Why was he in the race ... if he would
   vote for another – leaving himself bereft –?
It would seem strange – opposing ...
   himself – as the polls he left ...
When one goes against God and what is
   right – opposing himself – going the wrong route!

Advance to the Rear!

Many decisions in life to be made ... some
   frivolous and some staid;
At home or at work ... responsibilities follow
   in the wake.
But, not to, "waffle" but face up to what needs
   to be done – things don't just fade;
Courage comes from within – given by God –
   can never be fake.
The higher profile the job, the greater emphasis on
   responsibility – is laid;
By some quirk – many gain a position ... and
   then – no leadership take.

I've wondered and pondered many times ...
   this line – of thought;
If these politicians in power ... we hear so
   prone to talk, ...
Were the ones to bear Arms – and away from their plush
   way of life – were wrought;
Would their arrogance change – or would they
   still look stupid and balk?
It seems our soldiers' welfare is not ...
   with compassion, fraught.
Sending them to all parts of the world ... should
   have long ago come to a halt!

Politicians thinking only to make a name – ready
   to send soldiers ... others to blame;
Women and men – decisions to make ... when
   young men's lives are at stake.
In years past when it was their turn – many
   refused – war to them then ...wasn't a game.

If, when they were young – they had been as eager
     to go as they are to send – would good soldiers make!
Many did their duty – giving their all … those
     who didn't – their excuses are lame.
Now these same people so determined to police the
     whole world – have come to life – for humanity's sake!!

It seems the ones in charge … who refused – in
     their duty to go …;
Are ready to send our armies to the world's
     end … shedding life's blood.
First protection should be to secure our own
     shores –
Remember, "Pearl Harbor" – the surprise foe!
Would they be willing to go … those who – resisted
     before – their blood to mingle with the flow?
If they or their children were required to take
     part – instead of speaking out! – would speak so low …
For a coward even protecting our own shores, too
     much for them … their name "John Doe"!

Any life is important – someone else's as much
     as our own;
When decisions are made … just calling it the "Coward's
     Brigade" – require those who refused before, but ready
          to send;
To be the ones to make up the army – board a
     plane or ship – take up arms and be gone;
A foreign people – and country to protect – with
     no vital interest our own to defend;
If blood shedding and death were personal and of
     their flesh and bone;
A guarantee – more politicians would campaign
 and vote to keep our soldier boys home!!

Fight ... For What?

A soldier is trained to fight ... so many
    types of war ...
To be a true soldier deserves ... a bright untainted
    star –.
Suffering and pain ... over and over again ...
    yet again ...
Comrades in arms ... to the very end – always
    on the other must surely depend.

Torn bodies and lives – going through much
    to survive –;
Whose problem, the peace ...? the countries
    that refuse to jive!
Sending our boys away from home to battle-
    grounds ... with world renown –;
Is nothing less than ... a political ruse –
    and to our own peace so unsound.

The ones who are so eager for others to
    go ...
Should be first on the list of immediate
    foe;
Countries torn apart – upheaval of every
    sort ...
But, young soldier's lives – so endlessly
    are aborted, being "cut short."

Our soldiers are to be for protection of interest
　　at home ...
Not to send them all over ... the world
　　to wander and roam –;
Security and love of country and family
　　should be enough of a tragedy –
But, not send them away ... in other countries
　　to stay ...

Each country has its own responsibility ...
　　to care for its own ...
A war that has lasted for hundreds of years
　　over religion ... our boys shouldn't be on loan.
Sides so different, need work their differences
　　out –;
This part of the world – with much trouble
　　its own ... can't rightly turn it about.

What if when there's trouble here ... other
　　countries decided to interfere –;
Would those so eager to send our soldiers –
　　far and near ...
Begin to retreat ... hiding – hard to find –
　　cowards in kind –;
Letting other countries come to negotiate –
　　getting us in line – deciding how to bind ...
　　　what a debate!

Nostalgia and Romance

Tea For Two

Just getting home from college … my younger sister and I
   walked over to buy some tea –;
We made our purchase – when walking back across
   the bridge – someone hollered – two shooting turtles upstream.
Hearing the voices, we stopped to look – the taller one
   looked like a boy I knew from school – thought it was "that"
     boy…
When they walked on down to where we were –
   I thought: oh, my – I know him not – didn't want to seem mean.

As they came closer … when seeing my mistake – I
   let it be known – before more steps they would take …
Saying in a voice I thought sounded rather loud and firm – "I
   don't know you" – the older one answered – "Won't take long to
     get acquainted."
We told our names – the younger boy was his nephew –
   introductions all around – coming rather late –
The older and taller was in the Air Force – just back
   from overseas – on a visit to see his brother, who highly in the
     community rated.

He had on his khakis – white tee shirt – carrying a gun –
   a handsome fellow – standing in the July sun …
When he asked the question, "What was doing that night?" – when
   the answer was "Church,"
He said, "I'll go to church with you –
   I haven't been in awhile …"
My sister and I went on home with the tea – she was
   so peeved – a little mad at me.

She said, "I knew it couldn't be whom you thought –
    he has a job – is gone out of state" –
You see – I had been off to school and didn't know all this …
Anyway, about church time, up he drove – knowing
    where we lived, for his brother who knew us all – told him so.
We went to church – he went back to camp – we
    wrote everyday – never being late, falling in love – he said at
        first sight …

We were married in a little over a year … had four children, church
    has grown ever more dear …
God called him to preach His word – this he has
    done – for forty-eight years; many souls have heeded what they
        heard.
Over the years, much teasing about going to buy
    tea – by both him and me –
The way two people meet – is interesting indeed –
    never know which hearts will be forever stirred.

I thought it was a great compliment what he always said to me …
Had been around the world – many places – but, I was the
    prettiest girl he ever did see …
Now – he says the "same," but I tell him "his eyes see
    dim,"
But, he's pretty much the same to me –
    you see, my eyes too, see dim, and because of love for him.

Our Fifty-Second Anniversary
(Triolet)

It's our fifty-second Anniversary!
Our daughters sent us to eat to celebrate;
Eyes dim, ears dull ... hard to tell when others greet;
It's our fifty-second Anniversary!
He begged own pardon ... I admired my own dress;
Walls of mirrors confused both of us;
It's our fifty-second Anniversary!
Our daughter sent us to eat to celebrate.

For: Tena and Pam

Forever
(Cinquain)

I love
You ... I do! The
Years are more than three score;
Only Heaven will let me love ...
You more.

Anniversary Poem
For: Carl

Like Ivy
(Triolet)

Another anniversary …
It's fifty-two for us!
Through thick and thin, our love has been;
Another anniversary …
True love twines two hearts like ivy:
Love's spirit … the heart does renew;
Another anniversary …
It's fifty-two for us!

For: Carl

You're Mine!

You are my Valentine!
And have been for so long;
Many years gone behind ...
"Cupid's" bow proved so strong.

Arrow made two hearts one,
No longer ... separate ...
Perfect aim without a gun,
Where two hearts integrate.

I love you "Valentine ..."
I do with all my heart;
You'd have to say you were mine,
When joined by "Cupid's" dart!

For: Carl
With Love

Happy Anniversary
(Cinquain)

I loved
You from the start …
Life's mountains and valleys,
Bringing joy and hurt, have not changed …
My heart!

For: Carl

Love at First Sight
(Triolet)

Ah! Love at first sight!
Few know it can be true!
After years of married life, love's imagery is bright
Ah! Love at first sight!
True love will last through the darkest of nights.
But, would it take a chance if the troubles it knew?
Ah! Love at first sight!
Few know it can be true.

Always To Remember

He came when he had a three-day pass;
But, since he was stationed far away;
The time taken in travel was vast…
Still, we both looked forward to that day.

In spring, summer, fall or winter's ice,
When time for his pass, he would leave fast;
Heading for those Oklahoma Hills …
Time he got there his, "pass" almost past.

Such little time, it did seem so sad,
Coming so far …with the stay so short;
In school or teaching, I was so glad
To see him … with the clock, time's cohort.

When out of the Air Force, we married:
Soon to be fifty-three years ago
With the Lord's help, love has carried
Us through … and blessings He did bestow.

When we were young, God called him to preach –.
The highest calling to man in life,
Our home was blessed with children to teach
God blessed me, too ... being a preacher's wife.

We'll just take the time to remember:
If ever is the time we should forget;
Experience the longing, as it were,
The nostalgia, of when we first met.

For : Carl
With Love

Home and Family

Love's Strong Bonds

Love is of a solid base ... not just a
    gossamer fantasy –;
It reaches out ... knows no limits or
    bounds ...
Reaches out to the exalted spirit or to the
    lowly – of insanity –
Love isn't bought ... matters not what
    many have thought ...
True love doesn't smother ... it has to let
    one be free –.
To thoughts their own ... each independently
    wrought ...
Yet, reaching out across such distance and
    space – me to you or you to me –
Communicating in spirit because our
    thoughts are directed the same ...

Such understanding comes from true love –
    a blessing from God above.
Love seems to fill the air ... more to be
    desired than worldly fame.
You need not talk ... need not explain –
    just support and love – bonds remain;
Though we're kept busy ... with all life's
    aims –
Still, when opportunity affords ... though
    years separated and apart ...
That love and understanding we share
    remains the same.
No matter how far ... hearts so close in
    prayer and thinking.

Home

Home ... home for a visit at last ...;
Been a long, long time since all were home together;
Always hindered by circumstances ... obligations vast.
Finally worked out so it can be ... a serious matter.

We're all a little older, but, will never take note;
We'll be so busy on "news," catching up –;
Years have passed, but memories ... come by rote.
Always favorite dishes as we take time to sup.

So many memories for each, of home ...;
Associated with no other place on earth –;
It matters not how far or what direction one roams;
At home – each has his own place from birth.

Christ's teachings should be center of home with faith;
Learning the way of salvation by repentance when young;
With faith, accepting Christ as Saviour ...gift, not reward.
This teaching was to each ... on this Salvation hung.

Home is the place where teaching for good or bad begins.
Values are stressed and instilled or left ... ignored ...;
This help decides if in strength one stands or bends;
The right teaching at home brings many rewards.

Home ... homes so different – yet, to all the same ...;
The nostalgia ... so common remains –;
Yet, heartstrings ... tug always, but to a different refrain;
Home is home ... be it humble or luxuriating in riches and
    fame.

For: all Four

Some Remain

There remain those to whom family grows ever
   more dear ...
Values taught them in growing up ... not only ears,
   but hearts did hear –;
Never forgetting the closeness to father and
   mother and siblings while growing up;
Back in time when the whole family was home
   to sit down to sup.

None of this modern day ... of running here, there,
   to and fro ...
Time was spent together ... to work, though did have
   to go –;
Home was an important place ... whether large or just
   a little space, to children, husband and wife;
And regular worship in Church together ...was a
   way of life.

Holidays were enjoyed by the grandparents, uncles,
   aunts, nieces, nephews ... the whole family ...
Birthdays, Thanksgiving, Christmas ... all others,
   just any –;
A time for celebration and to enjoy games and
   family fun;
Picnics with outings ... where everyone was so tired
   at setting of the sun, when day was done.

Family closeness, … like anything worthwhile, needs
be cultivated to be …
Each sharing, caring, working, loving … doing their
best to see …
That the others have the love, care and attention
that's needed;
All for one … one for all … remains paramount and
always determinedly heeded.

No matter what age … everyone important … each had
a part …
Family gatherings never complete … until the last
one was there to start –;
Responsibilities were taught … so all could learn,
no matter the age;
With faith in the Lord … taught of His word …
preparations for the world outside … had to be
the gauge.

Part of Your Heart

Each member of a family has a part …
Their very own place in a loving heart;
Sharing their pain … discouragement that's sent;
Suffering with them … their heart rent.

You hope and pray things will turn about;
When turning to God … blessings on route …
Meanwhile, you continue to be concerned;
Waiting … yet hoping – while lessons they learn.

Remembering when they were young and small;
Couldn't talk … or even walk without a fall –;
While your heart continues to reach out …
With love, you wait … desiring increased faith …
    not doubt.

Busy, Busy, Busy!

A busy man! ... busy, busy, busy ...
   seems it can't wait!
No matter the hours in planning,
   usually end up late!
Getting bookwork done, in the "nick" of time
   with schedule worked out,
Is something which takes much figuring
   and turning about .
My conclusion ... planning so much, doesn't
   do much good!
Too many not working ... interfere –
   can't do what I would!

Needing a little quiet ... just disappear
   out of sight!
To get some much needed rest –
   which is my right.
Having my own dreams –
   the same as the rest;
Trying my patience ... need time with the Lord,
   to be at my best.
It always seems – not enough
   hours in a day;
Enough for work ... but none
   left for play.

Seems others have time for
family and friends;
Making their choice ... what seems best
for them.
What's good for others ... should be the
same for me.
Personal time for me ... the same as
other men!
When needing more strength, on the Lord
I depend.
What would I ever do without Him – He is
so Good – such a Dear Friend!

A Blessing

Such a blessing – to have the love of those at
    home;
No lacking in support and concern … when things
    take a bad turn.
All desiring to help … actually feeling buoyed
    up with love's network;
A family – holding forth in supplication and
    prayer – does of the Heavenly lurk.
You can always know – when you're in trouble –
    you aren't alone … .
For those concerned are heart of your heart …
    and bone of your bone.
Feeling God's care … having their love … while
    knowing God's on His Throne …;
Even when things are so depressing … and going
    so wrong!

There's comfort and ease … in the midst of
    trouble and pain;
Knowing the security of God's love … helps –
    strength to regain;
As we're gathered up in the arms of love … over so
    many obstacles, carried above –;
It's as if we are borne, on the wings, of a snowy
    white dove;
To heights we could never attain … but, with love
    and prayers …;
As we soar upward in spirit … to where natural
    man – never dares.
God has blessed us with the institutions of home
    and the true church;
To fortify us – when our lives become burdened
    with confusion – in life's search!

There are a Few

If fortunate enough .... to have a daughter or
    son;
Who proves a friend and from trouble doesn't
    run –
But, in conviction unmovable – in that which
    is right ...
We should pray – thanking God for them – as
    for right they do fight –;
Knowing each day ... must take a
    stand –;

Problems just don't go away as ... need standing up
    to again and again;
With never a thought to turn their back ... or
    run away –;
When principle's at stake ...becomes necessary
    to stay ...
There are days ... when others we may
    escape –;
But, ourselves, "NEVER" ... we're there when we
    awake!!

Staying true to the Lord ... there's always a few –
when troubles at hand ...
It always is best ... and to please God – faith is
what He demands –;
Character shows forth – for all to see – in many
a test.
True to self – friends, but God ... above all
else ...
When at peace with self – a quiet mind and heart –
with spirit free ...

Christ came that we might have life and it more
abundant be.
Loyalty ... without wavering – is a rare – enviable
trait –;
Such a person when found ... the devil does –
hate.
But, continuing to trust the Lord ... with His
strength given ...
Victory – is always His – at times sooner than later ...
all is by – His power driven.

Such Loving Help

We know our only help … comes from our Lord …;
God works through people to carry out His work here on earth.
He will give strength to those who obey – always a reward.
All who received Christ as Saviour … have a new birth.

It's so comforting to be supported by those who love and care;
Though we have the promise the Lord will never leave us –;
Such a loving spirit to have others our burdens to help bear …
With love, they share our pain and hurt – with hearts that are
    just.

You feel their love and concern … no matter the miles away;
The distance separating loved ones matters not – in the least …
Knowing their prayers are ever with you – come what may;
When God chooses to give relief – He has only just a little of
    his power to release.

Such loving help from family – doing what they can – praying,
    too …
Helps lift burdens – without their help – would bend one very
    low –;
But, with God's blessing – a family drawn by love and prayer –
    as refreshing dew –
When there is dedication of a family to God – you'll defeat
    every foe!

Whatever the trouble – no matter the depths of human
  despair;
Faith in God – loyalty to Christ ... loving care for those we
  love –;
There's nothing in which we can count God out – never to
  dare ...
What's hopeless to others – but not with the Lord – our
  strength's from above.

So many professionals in the health and medical field;
Depend only upon their own expertise, technology and latest
  medication;
The Great Physician – our Lord – is the only one who can
  heal ...
He directs the way to recovered health – defying all medical
  regulations.

The maniac of the Gadarenes – while cutting himself among
  the tombs;
When Jesus came that way – he turned to the Lord ...
As he turned to the Lord for help – the demons in his heart
  and mind – had no room.
The demons left – but even in his tormented mind he knew –
  in Jesus' help he would find healing and peace.

Getting Everything Ready

Getting everything ready ... for church – so
   much to do –;
Make sure all clothes to be
   worn – are as they should be.
So all the family can make a good impression –
   from that perspective – not have to rue ...
Each one making sure the others have
   all things together – they can see.

If as much time were taken to improve
   the spiritual part of man ...;
As is spent on readying the clothing –
   the mortal body's pride and plight ...;
To make a favorable impression
   on all made of dust across the land ...;
Frantic, at times, if everything doesn't turn out
   to look just right ...

What does God think – He who looks into the heart – and judges ...
   in His light ...;
Time spent before hand in study and prayer –
   prepares one for the service to follow –;
Much of the time – more time is spent
   in getting "things" ready – than getting things right –!
Perhaps, that's why so much of the time ...
   our audible prayers sound strange and hollow.

Eclectic

Fashioned Values

The student said, "I really love my, "mini" skirts";
Another replied, " I have, "many", but not, "mini";
For "many" of the, "many", "minis" look like shirts!
As to skirt ... "many", "minis", have hardly any!

Shorts invariably, come in various lengths, it seems;
There's walking shorts; length, somewhere around the knee;
They go from there, higher up, baring all they leave!
When the high-rise can't rise higher, they split the seam!

There's some so attired, when getting out of the car ...
Start pulling at the legs, to stretch, what isn't there!
So prevalent in summer, a good day it'll mar;
Embarrassed? It seems! As if they're out on a, "dare"!

"We've come a long ways, baby" – no place else to go!
Just to think! seeing an ankle, "exposed" was bad!
Bible teaches, women dress in, "modest" apparel;
It's best not sell, "values" for just passing, "fad"!

That which is highly prized, is never, "auctioned" cheap!
Purity and virtue, can never be bribed or bought!
When good, "moral values" aren't respected ... much to reap;
If trampled down, cast aside, hard to find when sought!

You Decide

"Trash it" from one … is to another a rare find;
Excited – one exclaims – "Did you ever see such a one?"
Trashed by one … seeing no value any kind;
One making the find – sees value when there is none.

"To each his own" – the saying goes – no one's the same;
Since this is true – your own self-esteem renew;
Be the best you can be – life isn't a game;
Interest one can have – many avenues to pursue.

Be yourself – maybe it's "trash it" – or "a one of a kind;"
You be the one to decide … which is true –;
Whichever it seems to you – let it be the measuring line.
God made us all – individuals – only one of you.

To yourself – but, most of all – to God be true;
When you do – life will be filled with such pleasure;
Living a life obedient to Christ – gaining God's approval;
Whatever the decisison – in Heaven should be the treasure.

Inside and Out

Nothing seems right ... everything looks wrong ...
    and many say is ...;
Being dissatisfied ... makes me nervous – always in
    a tizzy –;
An appointment for cosmetic surgery ... is already
    booked;
Forget the inside ... it's the outward appearance on
    which everyone looks.
There are many questions ... will there be a guarantee
    for improvement after?
Or after going to so much trouble ... will my looks
    still cause laughter!
At times, I'm persuaded ... that just might be the
    case ...
Mattering not what I have done ... my looks to efface,
    but, only to my face.
Where my chin is pushed in ... there's no doubt it
    should be out –;
And wrinkles need erasing ... not to another area
    pulled about.

It sounds so complicated ... not something to go ...
through just for fun ...
Thinking seriously ... as I check – just what can be
done.
Don't think just redoing my face will do ... when there's
much more needed to pursue;
Much word needs be done ... hips, waist, and ankles need
fixing ... you can see they do –;
So much is wrong ... there needs be a complete check
with overhaul ...
This is something new ... but, very true ... looks never
in the past mattered so much all can recall.
Many say real changes ... need come from the heart and
inside ...
That when heart and Spirit are right ... outward looks
they'll override.
The Bible does teach ... knowing Christ as Saviour, and
character counts the most ...;
But, when concerned with only outward looks and, "greed"
comes first ... no Spirituality or character to boast.

Raking Leaves

(De- Ja- Vu)

Raking leaves ... is good exercise – but
   of a good thing you can get too much –;
Leaves keep falling ... as the wind
   keeps flowing ...
Piles of leaves to put on the garden - and
   around the roses for mulch –;
Each morning – new leaves cover the ground –
   looking at the trees – they're going – going.

At times, it seems the leaves are so in abundance –
   will last longer than I ...
I'll just pick up the rake ... hoping soon
   there'll be a break –;
When all leaves ... having hung fast – their
   last ...
No more "exercise" – so glad to see the
   completely bare – once green trees –.

Next year ... we start anew – all over
   again ...
Excitement ... forgetting all the leaves when
   the trees begin to bud –;
Perhaps, I'll be in better shape when the
   leaves begin to fall ... by then –;
Sure to remember back when the leaves fall
   again – right here with the same old rake is where I stood!

Where My Money Went

Where my money went – I'd like to know!
Thought I was keeping up –but, away it went!
As if upon it, the wind did blow,
It seems I could own a mint!
At month's end still run low,
Perhaps, even without a cent!

Trying to account where money did go;
So much disappears without a hint.
Sure it's right – I'm my biggest foe!
Much better if money to myself I lent!
Charged high interest – payments just so!!
Then I'd have money regularly like rent.

Just pay myself – as others I always do,
Never running late – to have a clear slate.
It's an honorable way of life to pursue.
If to myself – payments wouldn't be late!
Plenty of money – not bills in lieu!
What a thought, just be my own banker – to date!!

Would do better than most people think,
If we'd treat ourselves as the bank.
We just sail along – until we almost sink;
Hmm! Could charge a penalty if we run late!
Never notice until bank account's lank!
No responsibility – we say it's just fate!!

Sick Abed

Sick abed – feverish – isn't any fun!
But, to get well, you must have rest;
This is always best, in the long run.
You twist and turn – yet, do your best;
While thinking – just to be out in the sun.
It's times like this – your patience tests!

The flu will spread – won't stop with you.
Don't spread your germs – be stern!
Cover mouth when you sneeze and cough – please do!!
Best, to practice the knowledge we learn!
Other's rights discern – they are important, too!
While you try new medicines – even, "old remedies" brew!

Take care and relax – a very good time;
To lie quietly, thanking God for blessings still.
Just think of all the times you felt fine.
Don't even have to take one nasty pill!
So just be thankful – don't overly pine.
Remember on occasion – even running uphill!

No matter how fretful or poorly you feel;
Better days are likely 'round the corner.
To pray and read our Bible will help us heal.
A peaceful mind is – never a boner.
Don't be impatient – though flu is real;
Germs here, there, everywhere – but, don't be a doner!!

Wired

Is that a UFO I see?
Most likely they'll beam me!
Wired to the hilt ... think I've been spied;
Here they come ... I'll be fried!

Braces on my teeth ... wire-framed eyes;
Plugs in ears ... no disguise.
I'm sitting with my lap-top ... yet −;
Surfing ... the Internet ...

No help to be found anywhere;
UFO'S ... cause a scare −;
I'm sooo afraid ... I'll say it's fun,
Find a phone and dial ... 911.

Did You Ever?

Did you ever secure a job and ... not know who did the
    interviewing or who hired you?
Records are kept with dates of hiring ... an application and
    resume is standard procedure ...;
Can you believe ... a high level job in government and not
    know who hired you or whom you answer to!!!
I don't believe one word of this ... and am convinced no one else
    does either.

The factory jobs ... farm workers ... the baker, even Santa Claus
    and the candlestick maker ...,
Know who hired them ... the salary they receive ... hours they're
    to work and the requirements –
There's so much illegal checking of files ... why not check the
    records so see ... tell us now and not later.
No need for all the questions ... pull the files to see ... surely
    even a novice would know the way things ought to be.

Seems so much interest in files ... why not check their own ... all
    these Congressional hearings – spending the tax-payer's
    money! ...;
Why not expect records to show what everyone is asking and
    seems no one knows.
A dubious situation ... if no records kept of hirings ... the IRS
    very doubtful will think that's funny.
More should be checked into and more should be expected ...
    since the, "two for one" in the White House are lawyers,
    politicians ... pros!

The First Leaf

At the mercy of all,
Don't come at beck and call;
    They decide ...
Trying to tell them when,
Crying, making such a din;
    They decide.

Not a leaf ... just a bud,
Just starting our in life;
    No one cares;
Certainly not as they should;
Nor to me as they could;
    All just stare.

To be fed on schedule,
When food is body's fuel;
    Isn't the same –
As to eat when hungry.
Appetite running free;
    Such a pain.

"Bath time," comes with the clock;
"Changing," time's when they mock,
    It's no fun;
Baby powder and oil.
As if encased in foil;
    Is the "sum."

Cutting nails, swabbing ears,
Will go on many years ...
    Have to wait;
They'll dress me as they like.
Like a girl ... I'm a fright;
    This I hated.

I can't walk ... neither talk,
So little I can't balk.
    That is sad;
Pushed around in a cart ...
I could drive at the start;
    Makes me mad!

The last leaf would be best;
At least, he could get rest ...
    That's the thing;
For feeding they awake –
It's not a piece of cake ...
    What they bring.

Last leaf sings his own tune;
To me, that's such a boon ...
    So wish I;
Singing to me, "off key";
While in their arms I lie ...
    Makes me cry!

Memories of the, "last leaf",
He's busy thinking of ...
    Though they're gone;
The "First Leaf" lies in bed.
Nothing in his head ...
    Not here long!

The last leaf has a cane;
If only I could fain ...
    Get to one!
I'd walk before I could –
They'd know before they should;
    I would run!

"Old Bough," maybe forsaken;
But, he shouldn't be shaken ...
　　　Takes his time –
He'll do as he pleases;
As he walks and wheezes ...
Is the "sum."
　　　He'll do fine!!!

Seems to me ... they should know;
To treat a, "bud" ... just so ...
Wish they would!
To make his stay with them –
Something pleasing ... just for him!
　　　Know they could!!!

Don't Kill the Messenger!
Change the Message!

When a person brings a message ... information which
   another person has sent to you ...
Don't be irrational ... if the message doesn't sound
   as you think it ought to do –;
Best to stay calm ... not refute the messenger ...
   saying it isn't true;
Until you check the message out ... keep your cool –
   using good manners in lieu.

If you prefer your own answers ... the message of the
   messenger you refute ...
Going ahead without the information ... your own plan
   to execute –;
A message is the precise words someone sent ... with
   nothing added or deleted to dilute;
Need wait ... investigate if the message delivered was
   the word sent ... best to remain mute.

Before knowing ... if you become so irate with the
   messenger ... accuse him of making a mistake;
And you keep trying the message with your own pre-
   conceived ideas to equate ...;
Then you find you've made a spectacle of yourself ...
   you listen ... but, too late –;
No one to blame, but, your own self ... it falls upon your
   own pate.

So Many Pictures

Everyone has pictures ... always collecting
    more –;
Best ones you bring into focus ... while the
    eyes adore ...
Are those filed deep in heart ... not just a
    few, but, scores;
Memory's tied to each picture ... not seen as
    before.

If one could only paint what the mind's eye
    does see ...
A beautiful picture would most all ... of them
    be,
Time has made clearer ... the important things,
    are free –;
Looking back ... mundane happenings grow dearer –
    you'll agree.

Though brush in hand, the artist could never –
    finish ...
Pictures would be rushed at him ... the last not
    diminished;
Thinking back of years gone by ... to life adds
    relish –
Memory lane is crowded ... with no need to –
    replenish.

Some Things Don't Change!

Weatherman said sunshine ... for sure;
But, haven't seen one ray ...
Plans made, but will have to endure;
Fog and rain for another day.

You'd think they would finally learn ...
So adamant not to be...
God in Heaven they need discern;
Decides if sun we see.

You'll notice ... the more sure they are;
The more confusion it seems;
So the Old Almanac ... just read;
The year's forecast ... forseen.

Accu-weather a misnomer –,
For there is ... nothing such ...
God can have all in derision.
Man thinks he knows so much.

There may be sunshine tomorrow ...
Might be better thus said;
"Could be sleet and snow ... clouds hanging low;"
Although we may be dead.

To Be a Rat

To be a rat ... means always to be on the lookout
    for a cat –;
It seem no matter where he goes, a cat comes
    creeping up ...
Cats all sizes ... colors and different kinds of
    breeds –;
Not watching only for cats ... but, sometimes
    even a frisky pup.

In the big building ... many people come
    and go –;
It's the courthouse – every country has one – where
    much legal business ... does fall –;
Rats are not excluded ... making their rounds –
    some running into a hole ...
Others standing straight and tall – from
    room to room – up and down the hall.

Many times both kinds of rats ... get caught
    up when out and about.
The little four-legged rats ...can only
    run into its hole and hide ...
Bigger rats ... in suits and hats – at times
    do get caught ... our courts prove that.
So hard, at times, to allow the Judicial System
    to work – and by the law abide.

Everyone wants the little furry rat ... gone –
    exterminated as a pest ...;
While much damage is done ... by rats
    of another name –;
All sorts of remedies are set forth to
    keep rats ... from spreading to infest ...;
What to do about the "dressed up rats" –
    some even aspire to fame.

When time comes – replace the questionable
    workers with a new face ...;
With ones – who have proven themselves
    not of the, "rat brigade" –;
Let the little four legged rats – find
    their place – hiding away from the human "rat race."
Then may come to the conclusion ... cats and
    dogs – not so frightening – their fears laid.

Case Dismissed

Having read of an argument ... to which belonged
    the spectacles – the nose or the eyes ...?
Was a funny situation ... as the argument they
    did pursue –.
Do you ever think – there's two eyes to keep the
    nose to size ...?
Eyes look down upon the nose ... superior in
    placement on you.

They sympathize one with the other ... the
    eyes water – the nose runs ...;
The nose runs ... the eyes water – one affects
    the other – but, each a separate one.
Spectacles would be of no use – if the nose
    didn't have a good bridge –.
The nose has no need of eye glasses – for it's
    sense is smell – can't change even in fun ...

At times, the eyes need help to see – but no
way of holding the eye glasses free –.
If you're on the jury – what's the verdict you
bring to answer …
Eyes versus nose … guilty or not – whose
are the spectacles – do all agree? …
The eyes look through – but the nose gains, too –
quietly – bridge in place – not having to run – making a face.

To keep down an argument – eyes not depending
on the nose's convenient bridge …
And spectacles not trespassing – crossing from
one side to the other –;
Then, "contacts" are the thing … they require
no sitting ridge;
The nose can't nose in – having no part –
case dismissed – the judge announced – nothing further!

What to Eat!

What to eat ... seems everything - turns
    to fat –
Certain things together – are said to
    produce a chemical breakdown –
If a nervous breakdown doesn't come first.
Those who stay on track ... hoping chemically
    To gain slimness back ... few to be found.

Who wants to continue eating cups of
    green beans – carrots and beets ...;
Exercising more would be much
    better – it seems ...
If ever to meet again – the two sides of the
    same coat ... quite a feat.
So thankful to be slim again – happy
    no more cupfuls of this and that, "plus" a smile that beams.

A few no-fat crackers ... a little bit of low-fat cheese ...
Oh, is it worth it? ... would like just
    a little more of something to eat –;
After losing the weight, meeting the set goal –
    finally accomplished – certainly no breeze ...
As weight came off ... appetite subsided – but need
    to be careful ... no final retreat!

Straightened Out

Being asked … to write a retraction …
Of a poem … I wrote before –;
For he apologized for his action;
Getting so upset … his feelings sore.

Here it is in writing …;
Having apologized … he wanted to know –;
If I had written a retraction …;
Showing he really wasn't a foe.

From now on when he's given a message …;
Sent from someone back to him -;
Perhaps, he'll reread this page …;
Remembering his action … not just a whim!!!

"DON'T KILL THE MESSENGER!
CHANGE THE MESSAGE!

Rhyme Over Reason

In writing, should one choose rhyme and not
    make sense ...
Or settle for more meaningful words
    at the rhyme's expense – ?
They say a poet expresses the truth – that
    would be so, if truth he buys and doesn't relent.
If a poet or – a would be one – caters to
    fashion in values – needs to repent.

God's values for the human race have never –
    done an about face ...;
Steady on ... trusting Him ... He'll supply the
    much needed grace –;
We must ... in living, writing, and rhyming,
    do the best we can ...;
Never forsake what's right to improve
    our standing, trying to shape our lives to rhyme
        with man.

It Matters Not

Which ear is more important – is there a certain one?
You have the right ear ... and you have the left ...
With which ear ... do you hear the best when it is done?
Both are for hearing ... sometimes one faces personal tragedy,
    being deaf.

Hearing loss may be in only one, or perhaps neither one –;
Or could be neither pick up the sounds as it should be done.
Just because you can't hear ... doesn't mean you're also
    dumb ...;
Lots of things to be learned – not only hearing, but other
    ways, quite a sum.

What if being jealous, the ears had a fight to the finish?
Envy ... because of one ear receiving the sounds first;
Would you be concerned if that were the reason, for hearing
    diminished.
Instead of picking up sounds together – just cancel the sounds,
    making it worse.

Be thankful you have the two – with which to do ...;
Two ears are sufficient – can get along without even two;
Other people have their duty to perform – same as you ...
Don't fret yourself – when others excel – don't get in a stew.

Others are necessary in the service of the Lord as ears on the
    body –;
It would seem one ear's job equal to the other ...;
Be thankful, if to hear with both ears you're able –;
Thankful we should be if God's work is furthered – even by a
    brother.

Killing Themselves To Stay Young

Many treatments for good health in the past
Is heralded now to be a detriment ...
Nothing to be done ... now but shadows cast –
On the "wanna be" young forever hint.

For years, it was the egg that got a bad rap,
And much proclaimed how bad the foods with fat,
Now nuts are said to help prevent disease,
Seems in all this, there's advertising sleaze.

Running was the ultimate for great health,
Everyone went out and bought jogging shoes,
Those who were poor or those who had great wealth,
Jogging has lost pace ... walking is the news.

Who can add one cubic to his stature?
The Scripture says, "Whether we eat, drink
Or whatsoever we do,
Do all to the glory of God."

Mixing It Up

Did you ever intend to do one thing
    and end up doing another …?
One man meant to brush his
    teeth obviously with toothpaste …
Inadvertently … picked up the
    Bryl-cream – oh, brother!
Someone else meant to use
    the spray deodorant … in haste –;
Picked up the hair spray instead
    of the other –;
A man in a hurry used shaving
    cream instead of deodorant-spray.
What about the one who sprayed his
    face with hair spray – then ran the razor over?
Spray cans aren't so widely used –
    they say because of pollution – perhaps to save face …;
Too many in too much of a hurry
    trying to catch up in the "rat race" …
Really that's more likely the reason for
    change … wrong choices – the base …
These are just a few mishaps, perhaps to
    make the case –;
But, more to it than the fear of the
    environment to deface.

The Flu Vaccine Has Flown

It's flu time and limited vaccine,
Many of our citizens denied ...
Heart patients and others at high risk;
Searching for some way to stem the tide.

Too many programs for our taxes!
Feeding many in third world countries,
Along with medical care and aid;
Some here pray – seeking help on their knees.

Our tax dollars could go for research,
Manufacturing our own vaccine!
Not leave our own people in the lurch;
While supporting others with our means.

We know God's Word teaches charity,
Not to the neglecting of our own;
Responsibility for family ...
The Bible teaches ... is widely known.

Worse than an infidel God calls him,
A person who doesn't care for his own (I Tim. 5:8)
Our country should not be neglected,
Homeland security ... then ... help them;

Our taxes should help us have vaccine!
Not depend on Britain, our Mother …
Much sickness, this winter we will see,
Vaccine tainted … a limit for others.

Oh, for politicians from here …
Or from just another country,
With "some" compassion to see our need
There are so many who would agree!

Charity SHOULD begin at home!

Old Age

Old age – can't hear, can't see … mumble
    when trying to talk …;
Creep along when trying to walk … back
    bent – all hunched over –;
Hands sore, fingers gnarled … arms
    crooked and bent – hair white like chalk;
Afraid of many things … careful of all –
    actions all meek and covert.

Ah! … but, old age is something more
    than being hampered by joints and pain …
As long as there's faculty of thinking
    and reasoning of mind –;
From years of living there's inventory in
    memories' bin prepared to last – pity disdain–;
A trip can be taken down memory lane –
    even in life's twilight – on which to dine.

Covering so may long winding roads –
    dark valleys along with the light catching hills;
Faith is renewed … in looking back we
    can see how in trials – God has seen us through.
True – our lives now are more sedentary
    and sedate …;
But, with wings of faith – through the
    atmosphere we soar – confinement our spirits eschew!

In Loving Memory

The Four of Us Know

We've all heard say those in Heaven,
Would not come back if they could,
But, the four of us know of one –
Our Mother, who would.

If and when her kids were small,
And needed lots of care,
She'd have forsaken those streets of gold,
And those mansions oh, so fair.

Though the golden shores would have beckoned,
Where the artesian waters flow,
She would have said, "Not now, Lord,
I must not, cannot go."

Another time, another day,
For I am needed most at home,
I know I must not stay,
For I cannot leave them all alone.

Little hearts and hands are depending,
On me, to take life's hurt away,
I must go and paint skies of blue,
And chase away clouds of gray.

She would have missed the angels singing,
And talking with the Saints of old,
To come back into a life of care and trouble,
For the little ones, you know.

She would have seen all the splendors of Heaven,
And taken only a moment to decide,
And crossed back over Jordan,
With its chasm deep and wide.

For when Heaven's gates were opened for her,
She would have chosen not to step inside,
And as much as her soul would have longed for Heaven
    and home,
Her love would have spanned the "Great Divide."

Written for: My Mother,
Maxine Spyres Hixon, my favorite poet
By: Pamela Hixon Rhea

November 25, 2004

For My Very Best Friend

Traveling back through the
    memory of time –
Brings wonderful thoughts in
    heart and mind.

Never a worry, never a care …
That didn't find Mother willing
    to share.

She'd kiss the hurts and wipe all
    the tears,
Not just once … but, for many
    years.

The more I've learned as older
    I've grown –
Reaffirms the love that Mother has
    shown.

Still, she took time to listen and
    hear,
Mattered not how small, to her
    it was dear.

She was more than my Mother,
    with support to lend –
She's dear to my heart … My
    Very Best Friend!

Written for: My Mother,
Maxine Spryes Hixon
By: Tena M. Hixon
October 6, 2005